I AM AN IMPURE THINKER

I AM AN IMPURE THINKER

Eugen Rosenstock-Huessy

INTRODUCTION BY

W. H. AUDEN

ARGO BOOKS, INC.

NORWICH, VERMONT

Contents

Foreword

"A GOOD WINE NEEDS no bush," and the same ought to be true for a good book. A foreword should be unnecessary. My reason for writing this one is that when *The Viking Book Of Aphorisms* was published, in which Mr. Kronenberger and I had included a number of quotations from Rosenstock-Huessy, a reviewer complained that he had never heard of him.

I first heard of him in, I should guess, 1940, when a friend gave me a copy of *Out of Revolution*, of which two chapters are included in this selection. (The whole, I am happy to say, has been re-issued as a paperback by Argo Books.) Ever since I have read everything by him that I could lay my hands on.

I should warn anyone reading him for the first time that, to begin with, he may find as I did, certain aspects of Rosenstock-Huessy's writings a bit hard to take. At times he seems to claim to be the *only* man who has ever seen the light about History and Language. But let the reader persevere, and he will find, as I did, that he is richly rewarded. He will be forced to admit that, very often, the author's claim is just: he *has* uncovered many truths hidden from his predecessors.

I was born and raised in England and always thought that I knew the history of my country between the accession of Henry VIII in 1509 and the accession of William III in 1688 fairly well, but it took a German to show me, what no English historian had done, the connection between the execution of Sir Thomas More in 1535 and the execution of Charles I in 1649, to explain the real meaning of the terms *Restoration* and *Glorious Revolution*, and why the revolutionary and permanent changes made by Cromwell had to be concealed and denied by calling the years from 1640 to 1660 *The Great Rebellion*.

Again, I am a poet by vocation and, therefore, do not expect to learn much about Language from a writer of Prose. Yet, half of what I now know about the difference between Personal Speech, based upon Proper Names, and Second and First Personal Pronouns, words of command and obedience, summons and response, and the impersonal "objective" use of words as a communication code between individuals, I owe to Rosenstock-Huessy. He has also clarified for me many problems of translation, for instance, the historical reasons why one cannot translate *Common Sense* literally into French or *Geist* into English.

Whatever he may have to say about God, Man, the World, Time, etc, Rosenstock-Huessy always starts out from his own experience as a human being, who must pass through successive stages between birth and death, learning something essential from each of them. For this reason I would recommend a reader of this selection to start with the two autobiographical pieces at the end. He will understand better, I believe, when he reads the others, exactly what the author means by his motto *Respondeo etsi mutabor* (I answer even though I have to be changed), and why he attaches so much importance to it.

Speaking for myself, I can only say that, by listening to Rosenstock-Huessy, *I* have been changed.

W. H. Auden

Editors' Introduction

BETWEEN 1920 AND 1970 over twenty books by Rosenstock-Huessy have been published in Germany and the United States. Yet the circle of his readers has been a small one. To date he has remained the private enthusiasm of two groups: his own students and the avant-garde among contemporary thinkers. Poets like W. H. Auden and Carl Zuckmayer, on the one hand, and theologians like Leslie Dewart and Harvey Cox, on the other, have sensed his importance.

In publishing *I Am An Impure Thinker* and a companion volume, *Speech and Reality*,[1] Argo Books is asserting its conviction that Rosenstock-Huessy's time has come: that he can move from private enthusiasm to public recognition and readership. The icy expanses of traditional philosophy, theology and natural science have begun to thaw and break up. A thinker and a doer who is not at home in the old categories is no longer an outcast but a leader.

Rosenstock-Huessy's life work and writings were foreseen by a man younger than he whose voice still rings out over our times. Before he was killed by the Nazis, Dietrich Bonhoeffer wrote that Christianity could no longer be interpreted in a religious sense and that modern man was moving toward a time of "no religion at all." It is toward such a time that Rosenstock-Huessy speaks. His work might be summed up as the discovery of a post-theological language: a language in which we can talk about the old concerns of theology. We can rediscover, for example, with Rosenstock-Huessy the "pragmatic significance" of the term "soul."

---

[1] Rosenstock-Huessy, Eugen, *Speech and Reality* (Norwich, Vermont: Argo, 1969). In this book Rosenstock-Huessy reveals his *method* of thinking and speaking. He contrasts his method based on speech with the mathematical or objective method which has dominated contemporary science.

With the exception of Chapters 1 and 11, the essays in this book have not been published before. The editors have made the selection from Rosenstock-Huessy's unpublished writings with a view to introducing the reader to the diversity of his thought. He is not an "impure thinker" by chance but to serve a particular purpose. His impurity is intended to redirect our thought, to give us a new orientation to our world.

Reorientation, indeed, is perhaps the best single word to describe what Rosenstock-Huessy is up to. His writings and life have been devoted to grasping the strands of history which led up to the World Wars and to reweaving from these strands a new fabric of thought and action which will enable us to cope with the changed times in which we live. As he writes in *The Christian Future:* "The two World Wars were the form of world revolution in which this new future reached into everybody's life. . . . The real transformation was made by the wars and it made the Great Society final. She is the heiress of State and Church."[2] Rosenstock-Huessy's books, including this one, recapitulate this quotation since they deal with the three major areas of human life: our history, culminating in the period of nation-states; our beliefs as preserved by religion; and our society, as revealed by social science.

Throughout Rosenstock-Huessy's works one finds these three areas of human experience rewoven in new ways. And two great themes appear again and again as we discover the underlying unity in his diversity: *time* and *speech*. As we come to appreciate what time, times and timing can really mean, and as we plumb the depths of human speaking we realize how Rosenstock-Huessy has indeed translated the old concerns of theology into a language that will make sense to future generations.

It may help the reader to recognize the way *time* and *speech* become this book's real subjects if we describe briefly in the following paragraphs how Rosenstock-Huessy interprets and relates these two great themes.

All his life our author's love affair has been with "the

[2] *The Christian Future* (New York: Harper, 1966), p. 5.

times." He is a passionate historian. He tells history as our own story. Over thousands of years history has made us what we are today. More, he brings back into our consciousness the great impact that our own future exerts on us, after centuries in which "space" was king in the minds of men. "Space" reigns where a mind, from its inner space, looks at the world, the outer space, to observe, measure, weigh; or where minds build great scaffoldings of thought. This is the world of the "pure" thinker; it is also the academic world. It teaches us to analyse but it knows nothing about life and death and does not help when "we are concerned with the survival of a truly human society" (p. 2).

Into this world governed by space the author brings back again the powerful times, not as slaves of space but in their own mighty influence over us, as past and future, bringing about our present. Under the impact of life we are "impure thinkers"; we have to change, to give in, to balance, and to respond to the unforeseeable.

The times' great vehicle is speech. The broad river of speech over the centuries links all generations of men, and the "languages" of the past still help weave our future. Such languages, the author tells us, are not French, Swahili, or Latin. These are but dialects of the spirit of man as it has been incarnated into languages. Names—Caesar, Cromwell, Lincoln, Einstein, and words—marriage, poetry, reformation, parliament, solidarity, have become our common language over the centuries. Speech has indeed to do with time: it survives those who speak, it bridges death, it is the carrier of the human spirit. We are all both heirs of speech and its testators. We cannot help but be.

Our author traces the origin of speech back into the distant past in "Tribalism," "Modern Man's Disintegration and the Egyptian Ka," and "Heraclitus to Parmenides." He reveals what is still alive of the old "languages" in our times. He tells us the story of the human spirit.

In Jesus, Rosenstock-Huessy sees the great teacher of time and timeliness. Christianity is not a religion but a process in time. Only for a certain period in our history was Christianity concerned with the growth of the Church and living within the Church. For the last millennium it has been spilling over into our secular world, forming and shaping it, and still doing so, as described in "The Reproduction of Government." Jesus was the first to trust completely the spirit that lives in the word and survives death. He did this "by simply speaking to twelve average men" as we are told in "When the Four Gospels Were Written."

Christ invested his life; he put his death before the life of the spirit. That is what we call faith. It is not a pious belief but a fundamental law of the human spirit. "In nature birth precedes death. In nature life tries to shun death. In the spirit death precedes life. In the spirit the founder's death guides his heir's lives" ("The Twelve Tones of the Spirit," p. 72). Spirit cannot survive death without faith. Faith, again, has nothing to do with Sunday schools; we need it for living since "we grow into society on faith, listening to all kinds of human imperatives." Faith has to do with time; it has to do with the future.

The reader may now be prepared for the radical translation of Christian faith into secular language which he will find throughout this book and in the wider realm of Rosenstock-Huessy's work. As you imagine what your children or their children may be able to say of their Christian inheritance, consider whether this radical translation is not what our times call for. Is it not what Dietrich Bonhoeffer meant when he foresaw a "religionless Christianity?"[3]

Freya von Moltke

Clinton C. Gardner

Norwich, Vt.
May, 1970

[3] Bonhoeffer, Dietrich, *Letters and Papers from Prison* (New York: Macmillan, 1962), pp. 163–164.

CHAPTER 1

FAREWELL TO DESCARTES[1]

THE YEAR OF HARVARD'S tercentenary, 1936–1937, was also the tercentenary of a great intellectual event. Three hundred years ago the rational foundations of modern science were established. It was then that the "*Weltanschauung*" which lies at the root of our modern universities was first put into a book. Its author had intended to write some comprehensive volumes under the proud title, *Le Monde*. But that philosopher, René Descartes, was dissuaded by religious dangers from publishing them in full, and limited his task to the famous *Discours de la Méthode*. In it the great idealistic postulate of the "*Cogito ergo sum*" (I think, therefore I am) was formulated, and therewith the programme of man's scientific conquest of nature. Descartes' "*Cogito ergo sum*" opened the way to three hundred years of incredible scientific progress.

When Descartes came forward with his "wondrous strange" Discourse, the scholastic type of university had long since been in decay. He replaced the principles by which medieval thought had been guided ever since Anselm's "*Credo ut intelligam*" (I believe so that I may understand), with his "*Cogito ergo sum*." Among the possible starting points for our powers of reason, scholasticism had singled out man's faith in the revealing power of God: Descartes seconded it with his no less paradoxical faith in the rational character of existence and nature.

[1] From *Out of Revolution, Autobiography of Western Man*, pp. 740–758. Originally published by Morrow, 1938. Third Edition published 1969 by Argo Books.

The *"Cogito ergo sum,"* for its rivalry with theology, was one-sided. We post-War thinkers are less concerned with the revealed character of the true God or the true character of nature than with the survival of a truly human society. In asking for a truly human society we put the question of truth once more; but our specific endeavour is the living realization of truth in mankind. Truth is divine and has been divinely revealed—*credo ut intelligam*. Truth is pure and can be scientifically stated—*cogito ergo sum*. Truth is vital and must be socially represented—*Respondeo etsi mutabor* (I respond although I will be changed).

Our attack on Cartesianism is inevitable since "pure" thought encroaches everywhere on the field of social studies. Historians and economists and psychologists cannot stand the idea of not being "pure" thinkers, real scientists. What a frustration!

I am an impure thinker. I am hurt, swayed, shaken, elated, disillusioned, shocked, comforted, and I have to transmit my mental experiences lest I die. And although I may die. To write a book is no luxury. It is a means of survival. By writing a book, a man frees his mind from an overwhelming impression. The test for a book is its lack of arbitrariness, the fact that it had to be done in order to clear the road for further life and work. I have done, for example, all in my power to forget the plan of *Out of Revolution* again and again. Here it is, once more.

Through man's own revolutionary experience, we know more about life than through any outward observation. Our ecodynamic moving through society is the basis for all our sciences of nature. Distant nature is less known to us than man's revival, through constant selection of the fittest, and through conscious variation. Man's memories of his own experiences form the background of all our knowledge of society and of creation.

Science, and history in its positivist stage, underrated the biological element in both nature and society. They took physics and metaphysics, measurable and weighable matter and logical and metaphysical ideas as the elementary and basic foundations on which to build our knowledge. By beginning with abstract figures in physics, or general ideas in metaphysics, they never did justice to the central point in our existence. For neither physics nor metaphysics can offer us any practical base from which to enter the fields of biology or sociology. Neither from the laws of gravity nor from the ideas of logic or ethics is there any bridge to lead into the realms of life, be it the life of plants and animals or of human society. Dead things are forever divided from the living; figures and ideas belong to the limbo of unreality.

We can drop the methods of the past. The schemes of that era, whatever they might be, were based on either physics or metaphysics. Some were subjective and some were objective; some were idealistic and some were materialistic, and many were a mixture of both. But they were unanimous in assuming that scientific thought should proceed from the simple facts of physics or general ideas. They were unanimous in assuming that either the laws of gravity or the laws of logic were primary and central truths on which the system of knowledge must be built. They all believed in a hierarchy with physics and metaphysics at the bottom, as primary sciences, and a ladder reaching upwards to the second and third stories of the house of knowledge. Once we see the cardinal fallacy of this assumption, Marx becomes as much the son of a bygone era as Descartes or Hume or Hobbes. They all look astoundingly akin. They all set out with abstract generalities on man's mind and on the nature of matter.

We renounce their approach to knowledge. "Thought" and "being," mind and body, are not the right points of departure for the masteries of life and society. Physics, interested in the mere being of abstract matter, and metaphysics, speculating about man's ideas, are at best marginal methods for dealing with reality. They do not touch the core, since they begin by investigating dead things or abstract notions. They are not concerned with the real life, either of natural creatures or of society. It is quite true that the universe is full of dead things and the libraries of men full of abstract concepts. This may *explain* the former presumption that, in studying a vast quantity of stones, gravel and dust, or an endless series of doctrines and ideas, one was attacking the substances which preponderate in the world. Yet this presumption remains a vicious circle. In a whole valley of stones and lava, one blade of grass is enough to refute a system which pretends to explore the grass by weighing and measuring all the gravel in the valley. In the same way, the presence of one living soul among the three million volumes of a great library offers sufficient proof against the notion that the secret of this soul is to be found by reading those three million books. Coal can be explained as the embalmed corpse of ancient forests; no tree can be explained by investigating anthracite only. Physics deals with corpses, and metaphysics with formulas from which the life has passed away. Both sciences are concerned with secondary forms of existence, remnants of life. The scientific treatment of these remnants may be very useful; yet remains a secondary form of knowledge. Life precedes death; and any knowledge of life in its two forms of social and cosmic life can rightly claim precedence over both physics and metaphysics. The two modern sciences of life, biology and sociology, must cease to take orders from the sciences of death, physics and metaphysics.

In a recent series of publications on biology, called "Bios" and inaugurated by the leading American, German, and English biologists, the first volume, written by A. Meyer and published in 1934, is devoted to this Copernican revolution. Meyer shows that physics has to do solely with an extreme case in nature, its most remote appearance. Therefore, physics can more fittingly be described as the last chapter of biology than as the first chapter of natural science. The same holds good for the social sciences in their relation to metaphysics. And the details which interest the sciences of death and abstraction are useless for the task which lies before the explorers of the life that goes on between heaven and earth, in the fields of economics and bionomics.

By the way, since the sciences under the spell of the old hierarchy of physics and metaphysics are usually characterized by the ending -ology (viz., sociology, philology, theology, zoology, etc.), a different suffix for the emancipated sciences of life would be convenient. When we speak of physiology, psychology, etc., we generally mean the sciences in their old form still biased by the physicist's and the metaphysician's errors. While speaking of Theonomy—as now commonly used by German thinkers—Bionomics—as the English usage goes—and Economics, we have in mind the mature and independent sciences of life which have become conscious of their independence from the sciences of death. Since we are facing the emancipation of these bio-sciences from "amalgamate false natures," a change in name is highly desirable to discriminate between their enslaved and their emancipated status.

The reality that confronts the bionomist and economist cannot be divided into subject and object; this customary dichotomy fails to convey any meaning to us. In fact, Mr. Uexkuell and the modern school in bionomics insist on the subjective character of every living object that comes under the microscope. They have rediscovered in every alleged "object" of their research the quality of being an "Ego." But if we are forced to agree that every It is also an Ego, and every Ego contains the It, the whole nomenclature of subject and object is revealed as ambiguous and useless for any practical purpose.

Sociologists like MacIver have taken the same point of view in the social sciences. The division of reality into subject and object is becoming worthless, ay, even misleading. It should be clear that in the fields of bionomy and economy it is an outrage to common sense to divide reality into subject and object, mind and body, idea and matter. Whoever acted as a mere subject or a mere body? The Ego and the It are limiting concepts, luckily seldom to be found in vital reality. The word "it," which may not give offence when applied to a stone or a corpse, is an impossible metaphor for a dog or a horse, let alone a human being. Applied to men it would reduce them to "cheap labour," "hands," cogs in the machine. Thus a wrong philosophy must necessarily lead us into a wrong society.

The four hundred years' dominance of physics inevitably leads up to the social revolution of the "It's," the "quantity" into which the workers are degraded by a mechanistic society. The politics and education of the last centuries proved a disaster whenever they tried to establish the abnormal and most inhuman extremes of Ego and It as norms. An imagination which could divide the world into subject and object, mind and matter, will not only accept the cog in the machine with perfect equanimity, but will shrink even less from the cold scepticism of the intellectual. His disinterested yet self-centred attitude, typical of the *déraciné*, will be thought of as normal.

Moreover, when humankind approaches a development by which one of its members, a class or a nation or a race, is to be enslaved and made into an "it," a mere stock of raw material for labour, or freed to become, as a group or class, the mere tyrannic Ego—a revolution will arise and destroy these extremes, Idealistic subject, the Ego, and materialistic object, the "It," are both *dead leaves* on the tree of mankind. Our survey of revolution shows that they are both insupportable extremes. The positions of Ego and It are deadening caricatures of man's true location in society. The great European family of nations was not concerned with the production or fostering of ideals or material things, but with the reproduction of types of the everlasting man, such as daughter, son, father, sister, mother and, of course, their combinations.

The abstractions and generalities that prevailed in philosophy from Descartes to Spencer, and in politics from Machiavelli to Lenin, made caricatures of living men. The notions of object and subject, idea and matter, do not aim at the heart of our human existence. They describe the tragic possibilities of human arrogance or pettiness, the potentialities of despot and slave, genius or proletarian. They miss the target at which they pretend to shoot: human nature. Though man tends to *become* an Ego and is *pressed* by his environment to behave like an It, he never *is* what these tendencies try to make of him. A man so pressed into behaviourism by awkward circumstances that he reacts like matter, is dead. A man so completely self-centred that he is constantly behaving as the sovereign Ego, runs insane. Real man enjoys the privilege of occasionally sacrificing personality to passion. Between action as an Ego and reaction as a thing, man's soul can only be found in his capacity to turn either to active initiative or to passive reaction. To veer between Ego and It is the secret of man's soul. And as long as a man can return to this happy balance he is sound. Our knowledge of society should no longer be built on non-existent abstractions like Godlike Egos or stone-like It's, but based on you and me, faulty and real "middle voices" as we are in our mutual interdependence, talking to each other, saying "you" and "me." A new social grammar lies behind all the successful twentieth century attempts in the social sciences.

King Ptolemæus' grammarians in Alexandria first invented the table which all of us had to learn in school: "I love, he loves, we love, you love, they love," Probably that table of tenses set the keystone into the arch of the wrong psychology. For in this scheme all persons and forms of action seem to be interchangeable. This scheme, used as the logic of philosophy from Descartes to Spencer and as the principle of politics from Machiavelli to Marx, is a grammar of human caricatures.

How far, in fact, does the "I" apply to man? For an answer to this question let us look into the Imperative. A man is commanded from outside for a longer time in his life than he can dispose of the "I." Before we can speak or think, the Imperative is aiming at us all the time, by mother, nurse, sisters and neighbours: "Eat, come, drink, be quiet!" The first form and the permanent form under which a man can recognize himself and the unity of his existence is the Imperative. We are called a Man and we are summoned by our name long before we are aware of ourselves as an Ego. And in all weak and childlike situations later we find ourselves in need of somebody to talk to us, call us by our name and tell us what to do. We talk to ourselves in hours of despair, and ask ourselves: How could you? Where are you? What will you do next? There we have the real man, waiting and hoping for his name and his Imperative. There we have the man on whom we build society. A nation of philosophizing Egos runs into war, a nation of pure "cogs in the machine" runs into anarchy. A man who can listen to his Imperative is governable, educationable, answerable. And when we leave the age of childhood behind us we receive our personality once more by love: "It is my soul that calls upon my name," says Romeo. It cannot be our intention at this moment to follow up the implications of this truth in all detail. The hour for such a discussion will quite naturally arise after the facts expounded in this volume have received better consideration by the general public.

However, one central result cannot be repressed even at this early stage of the " re-alignment of the social sciences" through the study of human revolution; and that is, that this study offers more realistic notions for man than the study of his mind or body. For the famous concepts derived from mind or body were, as we have said, "subject" and "object"; they are not to be found in healthy man in a healthy society. Man as a subject or as an object is a pathological case rather. The everlasting man as a member of society can only be described by reviewing the faculties which he has shown to us in the due process of revolution. He proved to be a beginner and a continuator, a creator and a creature, a product of environment and its producer, a grandson or an ancestor, a revolutionary or an evolutionist. This dualism that permeates every perfect member of the civilized world may be summed up by two words that fittingly should supersede the misleading "objectivity" and "subjectivity" so dear to the natural scientists. The new terms are "traject," i.e., he who is forwarded on ways known from the past, and "preject," i.e., he who is thrown out of this rut into an unknown future. We all are both, trajects and prejects. As long and in so far as our civilization follows a clear direction we all are sitting in its boat of peaceful evolution, and are safely trajected to the shores of tomorrow according to the rules of the game. Whereas whenever society shows no sign of direction, when the old boat of its institutions seems no longer afloat, we are challenged by the pressure of an emergency to take to an unknown vessel that we have to build ourselves and in the building of which more than one generation may be devoured. To build a new boat without precedent in an emergency, is the imperative of the revolutionary. Our trajectedness and our prejectedness, then, are our social imperatives. Their interplay is the problem of the social sciences. Traject is the evolutionary; preject is the revolutionary predicate for man.

We are aware of the bearing of this attack on Cartesian science, bound up as it is with Descartes' formula, *"Cogito ergo sum."* We take the full risk of leaving his platform forever. Thought does not prove reality. Modern man—and one need not turn to exaggerations like *Ulysses* by Joyce—is made into a bundle of nerves by thought. The modern man is pervaded by so many "foreign-born" ideas that he risks disintegration by thinking. The mind is not the center of personality.

Before bidding farewell to the *"Cogito ergo sum"* we should once more realize its power and majesty. This formula invited us all to join the army of research in its fight against irrational nature. Whenever a man was trained for the abstract Ego of the observer, our mastery over nature was at stake. On this unifying war-cry of "I think, therefore I am" man founded his glorious technical conquest of the "objective" forces and raw materials of the world. The George Washington Bridge across the Hudson is, perhaps, one of the finest results of this religious co-operation between rational Egos. Nobody can remain unmoved by its crystal-clear form. The alliance between all the thousands and millions whose co-operation was needed before man was capable of such a technical miracle is certainly inspiring. Or as President Coolidge said when he welcomed Charles A. Lindbergh home from his flight to Paris: "Particularly has it been delightful to have him refer to his airplane as somehow possessing a personality and being equally entitled to credit with himself, for we are proud that in every particular this silent partner represented American genius and industry. I am told that more than one hundred separate companies furnished materials, parts or service in its construction." And Lindbergh himself added: "In addition to this, consideration Should be *given the scientific researches that have been in progress for countless centuries.*" This army of man enlisted against nature under the password of *"Cogito ergo sum"* deserves our lasting support.

But among men, in society, the vigorous identity asked of us by the *"Cogito ergo sum"* tends to destroy the guiding Imperatives of the good life. We do not exist because we think. Man is the son of God and not brought into being by thinking.

We are called into society by a mighty entreaty, "Who art thou, man, that I should care for thee?" And long before our intelligence can help us, the new-born individual survives this tremendous question by his naive faith in the love of his elders. We grow into society on faith, listening to all kinds of human imperatives. Later we stammer and stutter, nations and individuals alike, in the effort to justify our existence by responding to the call. We try to distinguish between the many tempting offers made to our senses and appetites by the world. We wish to follow the deepest question, the central call which goes straight to the heart, and promises our soul the lasting certainty of being inscribed in the book of life.

Modern man no longer believes in any certainty of existence on the strength of abstract reasoning. Yet he is dedicated, heart and soul, to man's great fight against the decay of creation. He knows that his whole life will have to be an answer to the call. The short formula which we have proposed at the beginning of this chapter may be of some use to condense our whole endeavour into a sort of quintessence: "*Respondeo etsi mutabor*"—I respond although I will be changed. This formula which we propose as the basic principle of the social sciences, for the understanding of man's group life is as short as Descartes' "*Cogito ergo sum.*" Descartes assumed, in his formula, that the same subject that asks a question and raises a doubt solves the problem. This may seem true in mathematics or physics, though today with Einstein even this limited hypothesis has become undemonstrable. In any vital issue, he who asks and we who answer are widely separated. The problem is put to us by a power which far transcends our free will and by situations beyond our choice. Crisis, injustice, death, depression, are problems put to us by the power that shaped our miseries. We can only try to give a momentary answer, our answer, to the everlasting protean question. Our knowledge and science are no leisure-hour luxury. They are our instruments for survival, for answering, at any given hour of life, the universal problem. The answers given by science and wisdom are like a chain of which every link fits one special cog on the wheel of time. The greatest and most universal answers that man has tried to give, like the Reformation or the Great Revolution, even these, as we have seen, *were temporary answers,* and had to be supplemented after a century had passed.

The "I think" has to be divided into the divine: "How wilt thou escape this abyss of nothingness?" and the man's or nation's answer, given through the devotion of his whole life and work: "Let this be my answer!" "Man" is the second person in the grammar of society.

Having discovered, in every serious problem, the dialogue between the superhuman power that puts it and those among us to whom it appeals, we transfer the questioning I to regions more powerful than the individual. Environment, fate, God, is the I that always precedes our existence and the existence of our fellow creatures. It addresses us: and though we may perhaps voice the question, we are no egos in serving its mouthpiece. Persons we become as addressees, as "you." We are children of time and the emergency of the day is upon us before we can rise to solve it.

Whenever a governing class forget their quality of addressees, a suppressed part of mankind will raise its voice instead for an answer. Society shifted from an unsupportable dualism of haughty Ego and suppressed It into its proper place as God's addressee at the point of outbreak of every great revolution. A new psychic type took over the part of answering the question of the day whenever a province of Christianity was denied its own proper voice. When Italy was a mere tool of the Holy Empire, as in 1200, when Russia was an exploited colony of western Capitalism—as in 1917—a new sigh was wrung from the apparent corpse: and no Ego, but a new appealable group was born. No governing class ever survives as a mere self-asserting Ego. It will always survive by responding to its original claim as God's "you."

Nations are grateful. As long as a shred of the original problem is before the nation and as long as the members of the governing group show the faintest reponse to it, nations tolerate the most atrocious eccentricities in a perfect patience. This patience and gratitude may truly be called the religion of a nation. When a man—or a nation or mankind—wishes to be re-born, whether from too much solitude or out of the crowd, he must leave both the study of the Platonic thinker and the machinery of modern society behind him, and become an addressee again, free from egocentric questions and from the material chains of the It. In our natural situation, that of being an addressee, we are neither active like the over-energetic Ego nor passive like the suffering under-dog. We are swimmers in a buoyant and everlasting medium. The dawn of creation is upon us, and we await our question, our specific mandate, in the silence of the beginnings of time. When we have learned to listen to the question and serve towards its solution, we have advanced to a new day. That is the way in which mankind has struggled forward, century after century, during the last two thousand years, building up the calendar of its re-birthdays as a true testament of its faith.

The responsibility of inventing questions does not rest on the living soul. Only the devil is interested in bringing up superfluous and futile problems. Rightly, *Tristram Shandy* begins with an outburst against the "If's." The real riddles are put before us not by our own curiosity. They fall upon us out of the blue sky. But we are "respondents." That is man's pride, that is what makes him take his stand between God and nature as a human being.

Thus our formula has been given in three simple words: *Respondeo etsi mutabor*, I answer though I have to change. That is, I will make answer to the question because Thou madest me responsible for life's reproduction on earth. *Respondeo etsi mutabor:* by self-forgetting response, mankind stays "mutative" in all its answerable members. The "*Cogito ergo sum*" becomes one version of our formula, that version of it which was most useful when man's path opened up into the co-operative discovery of nature. In the person of Descartes, mankind, sure of the divine blessing, decided on a common and general effort, valid for all men, that would transform the dark chaos of nature into objects of our intellectual domination. For the success of this effort, it was necessary to cast the spell of the *Cogito ergo sum* over men to overcome their natural weaknesses and to remove them far enough from the world that had to be objectified. "*Cogito ergo sum*" gave man *distance* from nature.

Now this distance is useful for a special phase within the process of catching the questions and pondering over the answers and finally making the answer known. For the phase during which we *doubt,* we are sure of nothing but our thought; for that phase, then, the Cartesian formula was fortunate indeed. And since, in natural science, this phase is the most essential, natural scientists thought mankind could live on this philosophy at large. But we know already that the *expressing* of truth is a social problem by itself. In so far as the human race has to decide today on a common effort of how to express or represent truth socially, the Cartesian formula has nothing to say. And the same is true about the *impression* of truth on our plastic conscience. Neither the centuries that prepared and finally produced Descartes nor we post-War people can found our common international and interdenominational efforts on a formula that says nothing about the dignity of impressions and expressions, of learning and teaching, or listening and speaking to our fellowman.

The centuries of the clerical revolutions were concerned with giving us the good conscience and the certainty of the illumination on which Cartesius was able to found his appeal to the general reason in every one of us. They had to study the problem of *impression,* i.e., how man can learn what to ask from life. For that purpose, they had to establish another kind of distance within the thinking process. And the establishing of his kind of distance had to precede that secondary distance between subject and objects as established by Descartes. If Scholasticism had not done away with all the local myths about the universe, Descartes could not have asked the reasonable questions about it. In order that man might become able to think objectively at all, he had to know first that all wishful thinking of our race was outwitted by a superior process that originated and determined the part played by ourselves in the universe.

The real process of life that permeates us and gets hold of us, that imperils us and uses us, transcends our off-hand aims and ends. By revering it, we can detach ourselves from our fear of death, and can begin to listen.

As a principle of efficient reasoning, this detachment was transferred into philosophy by the greatest English philosopher, Anselm of Canterbury, in a sentence rivaling with the Cartesian in conciseness: *"Credo ut intelligam"* is the principle distancing men from God in their intellectual practice. We might translate the Latin (which literally means: I have faith in order that I may come to understand) in our terms: I must have learned to listen before I can distinguish valid truth from man-made truth. This, again, turns out to be but another version of our proposed formula in its triangular relation. In Anselm's statement the emphasis is on the hearing, as the organ for inspiration by truth. In Cartesius', it is on the doubting as the organ for transformation of this divine truth into human knowledge. In our phrasing, the emphasis shifts once more, and now to the process of making known, of speaking out at the right time, in the right place, as the proper social representation. We no longer believe in the timeless innocence of philosophers, theologians, scientists; we see them write books and try to gain power. And this whole process of teaching again needs the same century-long self-criticism applied by Anselmists and Cartesians to the processes of detaching us from God and from nature. In society, we must detach ourselves from our listeners before we can teach them.

Both the *Credo ut intelligam* and the *Cogito ergo sum* worked very well for a time. However, finally the *Credo ut intelligam* led to the Inquisition and the *Cogito ergo sum* into an ammunition factory. The progressive science of our days of aircraft-bombing has progressed just a bit too far into the humanities, precisely as theology had dogmatized just a bit too much when it built up its inquisition. When Joan of Arc was questioned under torture, her theological judges had ceased to believe. When Nobel Prize winners produced poison-gas, their thinking was no longer identified with existence.

Our formula *"Respondeo etsi mutabor"* reminds us that human society has outgrown the stage of mere existence which prevails in nature. In Society we must respond, and by our mode of response we bear witness that we know what no other creature knows: the secret of death and life. We feel ourselves answerable for life's "Renaissance." Revolution, love, any glorious work, bears the stamp of eternity if it was called into existence by this sign in which Creator and creature are at one. "*Respondeo etsi mutabor*," a vital word alters life's course and life outruns the already present death.

The Survival Value of Humor

Let us turn a last time to the venerable Descartes, our adversary, the great seducer of the modern world. In his booklet on method, he seriously, without any trace of humor, complained that man had impressions before his mind developed to the full power of logic. For twenty years, so his complaint runs, I was impressed confusedly by objects which I was unable to understand. Instead of having my brain a clean slate at twenty, I found innumerable false ideas engraved upon it. What a pity that man is unable to think clearly from the day of his birth, or that he should have memories which antedate his maturity.

Have these naive confessions of the demigod of modern science, the inventor of the mind-body dualism, met with the only success that they deserve: unending laughter? This brings up the serious question of what the omission of laughter, or its application, mean in the evolution of science. Scientists seem to be unable to grasp the folly of Descartes' remark. Common sense, however, acts on the principle that a man who fails to apply laughing and weeping in the discovery of vital truth simply is immature. Descartes is a gigantically expanded adolescent, full of curiosity, loathing his mental childhood, and frustrating his mental manhood.

Descartes wished to have man's plastic age erased. He wished to transform man from a plastic preject thrown into life and society so that it might be impressed and educated, into an empty subject to be filled with objectivity. This amounts to saying that the human mind should decipher only the impressions made on those parts of the world that are outside himself. Consequently the scientists today, for they all represent the practice of Cartesianism, think that they must not be impressed themselves, that it is their duty to keep cool, disinterested, neutral and dispassionate. And they try hard to develop this lack of humor. Their inhibitions and repressions are such that they give vent to their passions for trifles, and most unconsciously, only because they do not dare to admit them as the greatest capital of human investigation.

The more a man represses the impressions made upon himself, the more he must depend, in his orientation and conclusions, on vestiges and impressions made by life on others. He is suppressing some of the evidence of the world he is studying when he claims to work with pure mind. Let us compare very briefly the physicist or geologist, the biologist or physician, and our own economics and "metanomics" of society. Then it will become clear that they all form a logical sequence.

Geology depends on impressions made by floods, earthquakes, volcanoes. The mountains tell the story of their oppressions and rebellions. The outstanding data of this science of Mother Earth are those furnished by the most violent impressions that mark an epoch in evolution.

Turning to medicine, we easily observe that a physician will not recommend a new drug before some living beings have tried it out. The serum or antidote becomes of interest when it leaves a real impression on or in a living organism.

All true sciences are based on impressions made on parts of the world, on stones, metals, plants, animals, human bodies, from atom to guinea-pig.

Very well, if the impressions made on stones have brought forth a special science, that of stones, and if the impressions engraved in bodies have built up modern medicine and biology, then the impressions that are powerful enough to shake our minds must be of greatest scientific fruitfulness. Aping, however, the natural sciences, the brahmins of the knowledge of man boast of their own neutrality and impassive indifference to the issue. No science being possible without impressions, they turn to an artificial laboratory where they produce effects on guinea pigs, and substitute the experiences of the guinea pigs for their own.

The truth is that the great Cartesius, when he obliterated the impressions of the child René, maimed himself for any social perception, outside natural science. This is the price paid by any natural scientific method. As far as it is applied, and neutralizes the geologist or physicist or biochemist, it obliterates their personal social and political experiences. Hence, the sciences develop a habit which is disastrous for the social thinker.

No scientific fact may be verified before it has made an indelible impression. The terror of revolutions, war, anarchy, decadence, must have made an indelible impression before we can study them. "Indelible" is a quality that differs widely from "clear." In fact, the more confused and complex and violent the impression, the longer it will stick, the more results will it produce. A revolution, then, is the most important fact for understanding, because it throws our minds out of gear. By definition, a revolution changes the mental processes of man. The scientists who sit in objective judgment before they are overwhelmed simply disable themselves for their real task, which is to digest the event. They do not expose their minds to the shock. In other fields of life this is called cowardice.

The cowardice of the social thinker who denies that he is impressed and shell-shocked personally by a revolution or a war-scar, makes him turn to statistics describing the buttons on the uniforms of the soldiers, or makes him list the botanic names of the trees on the parkways where the insurgents fell. The impressions that matter, as they are given, for instance, in Tolstoy's *War and Peace* (his own fears, hopes, etc.), he is at a loss to admit: and so he looks for second-rate impressions that are too funny for words. And again, nobody dares to laugh.

Hence, scientific progress in the social field depends on the regulating power of humor. Humor precludes wrong methods by simply ridiculing them. *Le ridicule tue.* And as much as chemists need laughing gas, we need, to exclude the pretensions of impassionate thinking, a strong dose of humor. If we could place mirth on the throne of society, the war-scar that produced this volume would finally have vanished.

My generation has survived pre-War decadence, the killing in the War, post-War anarchy, and revolutions, i.e., civil war. Today, before anybody awakens to conscious life in this narrowed world, unemployment, or airbomb-strafing, or class-revolutions, or lack of vitality, or lack of integration may have cast the die of his fate, and stamped him forever. We daily emerge out of social death by a miracle. Hence, we no longer care for Cartesian metaphysics which lead man's mind beyond his physical death in nature. We are groping for a social wisdom that leads beyond the brutal "nomical" facts of economics and the monstrosities of the social volcano.

As a survivor, man smiles when realizing how narrowly he has escaped. This smile, unknown to the dogmatic idealist or the scientific materialist, twists the face because a human being has survived danger and therefore knows what matters. Humor illuminates the inessential. Our modern sciences, on the other hand, die from the carloads of inessentials that are dumped daily on the student's brain. In modern society the idea prevails that science is on the increase in bulk. They are adding, adding, adding to the mountain of knowledge. The man who survives is starting, starting, starting. For he is recovering his mental powers after a social catastrophe. And he looks into the blossom of a flower with greater surprise and delight at seventy than when he was a child. The survivor in us, though he may lose in curiosity, gains in astonishment. The "metanomics" of human society are tokens of the surprise that man survives. Beyond, that is to say "meta," the "nomical," the all-too-mechanical brutalities of social chaos, "metanomics" arise. They constitute the gay knowledge that Nietzsche was the first man to acclaim as *"gayza Scienza,"* mirthful science. The results of "metanomics" form the frame to the joyous exultations of life; they allow life to be resuscitated and revitalized whenever it has spent itself. The results of a "gay science" do not neutralize life, they protect its exuberance. They bind together, in a common mirth, the survivors and the new-born. Thus, "metanomics" has its definite place in the autobiography of the race. Whenever the survivors have experienced death they are able to instil their dearly bought humor into the vigorous joy of youth. Never did mankind acquire a common knowledge by storing it away in libraries. Tell me, however, that you are willing to experience your life as a sentence in humankind's autobiography, tell me how far you share responsibility with the blunderers of the past, and when you have shown me to what extent you are capable of identification with the rest of mankind, I shall know whether your knowledge is survival knowledge, "metanomics" of society as a whole, or merely your private metaphysics.

My generation has survived social death in all its variations, and I have survived decades of study and teaching in scholastic and academic sciences. Every one of their venerable scholars mistook me for the intellectual type which he most despised. The atheist wanted me to disappear into Divinity, the theologians into sociology, the sociologists into history, the historians into journalism, the journalists into metaphysics, the philosophers into law, and—need I say it?—the lawyers into hell, which as a member of our present world, I never had left. For nobody leaves hell all by himself without going mad. Society is a hell as long as man or woman is alone. And the human soul dies from consumption in the hell of social catastrophe unless it makes common cause with others. In the community that common sense rebuilds, after the earthquake, upon the ashes on the slope of Vesuvius, the red wine of life tastes better than anywhere else. And a man writes a book, even as he stretches out his hand, so that he may find that he is not alone in the survival of humankind.

CHAPTER 2

THE SOUL OF WILLIAM JAMES[1]

I. On The Significance of The Term "Soul"

THE PLACE: LA VERDETTE, a modest country mansion near
Avignon, the city of medieval Papacy, in southern France. The
time: the end of August, 1903, five months before the Russian
fleet was attacked at Port Arthur by the Japanese fleet, and
sixteen months before the First Russian Revolution broke
out. So, in August 1903, the ideas of the French Revolution
drew to a close. And truly, their era was embodied in the old
man at La Verdette who filled the last days of his life with
sublime conversations on three topics: Freedom, Justice, and
the Fall of France. That sage was Charles Renouvier, "the
director of French conscience for a quarter of a century," "the
inspirer and teacher" and converter of William James.

Renouvier was 88 years old. On his deathbed, he confessed
his sadness: "The French may cease to be a nation; a Prussian
General may come to rule them. We await the beginning of
an intellectual and moral decadence which will lead us quickly
to a new night of the spirit as well as of the heart. . . . Mech-
anisms and gadgets made by the work of man will make life
easier, and will make man the worker proud of himself; no
serious literary, philosophical, scientific culture will remain.
This night may last long." William James had proposed that
this Frenchman who thus spoke on the last day of his life
should be a candidate for the Prussian Academy of the Sci-

[1] An address delivered on the 100th birthday of William James, January 11, 1942, at Dartmouth College.

tremble lest I paint a bald James though his hair rippled, and a solemn soul, though he rocked with laughter. But if this moment, in this country and in our whole world, demands proof of souls, nobody better than James himself can offer it.

In times of crisis, the term "soul" is of "pragmatic significance" because it signifies our power to survive mortal fears. When Thomas Paine exclaimed: "This is a time that trys men's souls," he did not mean men's bodies or men's minds. And we know it. And at the end of his speech before Congress, Winston Churchill suddenly dropped all pretense of being slangy, witty, superior, and struck at his audience suddenly: "If you will allow me to use other language." And then he did use their language indeed. For he continued: "I will say that he must indeed have a blind soul who cannot see that some great purpose and design is being worked out here below, for which we have the honor to be the faithful servant."

These words are semantic blanks for the logical positivists; they swept Congress off their feet. Neither bodies, athletic bodies, nor minds, the most subtle minds, perceive honor, faithfulness, service, the things which count in war. Soulless men could not prevent the Japanese at this moment from being in San Francisco or the Germans from hovering over New York. Men could not go to war if they had no souls. For war is a struggle for the survival of others than ourselves, in honor, faith and service, a struggle for a purpose which is not of our making and which can only be accepted after we have thrown off mortal fear. In the peaceful years between 1865 and 1910, William James held that "however rare heroic conditions might be in fact, the true creed must be adapted to them. For only the extremes of heroic action and belief cover the whole range of life." "Heroic" signifies the absence or the neglect of the fear of losing our lives. And so I now turn to a "more serious consideration" of the soul of William James.

II

You have heard of William James' work in the field of science. He ruined his health at this work. Work was the gospel of his age. "It works" was the famous catch phrase of pragmatism itself, the school to which James seemed foremost to belong. The vocabulary of labor—toil, work, production, results—colored the industrial era. James paid his toll to the religion of his time. Compared to Montesquieu, who composed his *Esprit des Lois* in indescribable nonchalance and insouciance compared with any man of the eighteenth century, William James worked like a laborer in a modern tool shop.

James did his hard work in the service of science, in the classrooms of a university and of a great college. All work has its code of specialization, and this code requires resignation. In the industrial system work is not done by the whole man. James suffered more than any man I know from the routine of work and from its destruction of wholeness, yet he accepted the code; he resigned himself even when he hurt his own subject. For instance, in his "Will to Believe," he argued about the energy called "faith" in such a manner as to exasperate John Jay Chapman, who blurted out to James: "The course of reasoning, or say state of mind, of a man who justifies faith by the consideration you mention, is well enough. But he'll never convey it, arouse it, evoke it—in another." There are forces in life which are murdered when they are not conveyed, aroused, evoked in others. And the gospel of objective work in science does not allow for growth, expansion, transmission of the powers of man. You might expect that James would have contradicted Chapman's accusation that he falsified these forces simply by bringing them to a standstill. Not at all. Humbly, James replied: "Damn me, if I call that faith, either. It is only calculated for the sickly hotbed atmosphere of the philosophic, positively enlightened, scientific classroom. To the victims of spinal paralysis which these studies superinduce, the . . . treatment, although you might not believe it, really does good."

Through resigning himself to the "atmosphere" of scientific work, James the expert won the admiration and love of his psychological and philosophical confreres. Taking upon himself the limitations of the gospel of work, joining hands with all the millions who in those decades increased and expanded our means of intellectual and material production, he became the exponent of his era, the outstanding thinker of America at the turn of the century.

However, mere work would not have made him such a leader, if he had not tempered the iron age of work by a glow from another quarter. He was a gentleman through and through. And he could get very angry at plebeians. The gentleman, the man of independent means, and the hard-working plebeian do not go together easily. In work, things have to get done. There is a ruthlessness in work, as in any objective activity of man. How can it be mitigated by qualities which stem from social intercourse? Work can be done in a gentlemanlike fashion, even in modern society, by the most scrupulous respect for any other man's contribution to the work. James became famous for cultivating this trait to a sublime degree. Although not a team worker like one in a modern laboratory, he breathed the spirit of a team. He saw greatness, usefulness, memorability, everywhere. In him two opposite types were fused: in him were perfectly united the natural type of his age, Meunier's worker, and the social type of his age, the sensitive gentleman.

By such achievements, we obtain a passport throughout one time only. But James is still with us. How is this possible? When Stanton said of Lincoln: "Now, he belongs to the ages," he linked his hero with times, people and manners far distant. In a similar manner, we celebrate our hero today because he is linked to people of the past and of the future, outside his code of work or manners. James' roots went down in the soil of time before the great French Revolution; the branches, if I may say so, of his thought will stretch beyond the coming peace conference. Though a citizen of the peaceful era—between our Civil War (that last wave of the French Revolution) and the next great wave of the two World Wars,—William James belongs to the ages. In order to do him justice, we must connect the worker and gentleman of 1900 with the non-conformist and free thinker of the 18th century and the soldier of the 20th century.

Since you all know hard work and fair play, you can all

identify yourselves with the worker and gentleman in James. You sympathize perhaps less readily with the non-conformist or the soldier. The free thinker in James, at least, is no stranger among us.

Like the "enlightened" men of the 18th century, James possessed an uncanny and sometimes absurd curiosity about anything and everything under the sun. He also was quite sure— at least most of the time—that all that man could say dealt with "things" in the universe. It was left to the generation after James to show that man and the world and God are not reducible to each other, and that they can not even borrow language from each other. Yet James belonged, with Bergson, to the generation that sought deliverance from mere world-liness and mere things. Though he actually defined man as "a thing which," he at least disliked that state of affairs.

The free-thinker is often confused with the non-conformist. But the two differ as widely as the worker and the gentleman. The free-thinker, like the worker if left to himself becomes ruthless; he feeds on his objects like a bird of prey. The non-conformist emigrated to America for his conscience' sake. He created there a non-conformist environment—a church, a con-gregation—at terrible expense: the non-conformist incarnated himself in his every breath and act and step, in the home, the school, the meetinghouse. Is William James such an "expensive" thinker and professor of his faith?

Listen to the words he asked to have repeated to his son: "Tell him to live by yes and no, yes to everything good, no to everything bad." And: "I can't bring myself to blink the evil out of sight, and gloss it over. It is as real as the good; and if evil is denied, good must be denied, too. It must be accepted and hated and resisted while there is breath in our bodies." The non-conformist knows that evil exists (a fact which the "enlightened" age so often forgot), and that evil increases automatically. Inertia, laziness, cowardice, death, are self-multiplying. The Methodists, Baptists, Quakers, Shakers, the Jehovahs Witnesses, all agree in this, that good "*is*" not, except by propagation; it is not in any man, but originates only between teacher and student, between father and son, between a Renouvier and a James.

Exactly as children are begotten, so the gifts of the spirit, the fertility of goodness, the contagion of enthusiasm, the fecundity of thought, the influence of authority, are interhuman processes which spring to life only between people. No man is good. But the word or act that links men may be good. And by link-work evil has to be constantly combatted. Whereas the dogma of hard work and the pride of free-thinking ignore this constant reproduction of the good, and leave the arousing, evoking and conveying of goodness to accident, the non-conformist in James checked the abnormal curiosities of the free-thinker, and the reckless experimentation of the worker.

This power came to him from a rare relation to his family. Of his father, our hero had this to say: "He was a religious prophet and genius if ever there was one." Without anything else to do, Henry James senior poured out a whole original system of theology in home and family. For forty years, William James and his brothers and sisters were exposed to an inspirational pressure of unique volume. Speech and thought came to him not as the individual gifts of an upstart but they entered him as they enter or should enter, all of us, as rays from the radiant crown of a gigantic family conversation. Out of this cone of rays, William was the ray which fell upon philosophy. His father's theological refraction still has a future. It seems to me that because God was the most certain reality to James senior, William could overemphasize the world and its naturalness and could make extreme statements like "the thing which" when speaking of Hamlet or, equally horrible, that "the universe engendered our intelligence."

In this sentence and in many others, he gave man over to the world too completely, in line with the American secular tradition. But his father's freedom from the world came to life in him again through Renouvier, and he checked himself by interpolating freedom, novelty and goodness into this man-engendering universe. In an era of factory pragmatism, of more means for the sake of more means, James remained free to

resist trends, to combat tendencies. And when the era of fever-
ish, ruthless work also began to destroy the fiber of the inten-
sive groups built up by the non-conformists in family, church,
and small minorities—when a coarse nationalism replaced all
the more delicate groups—James stayed on the side of the
small "oozing capillaries" between persons.

III

Against the madness of nationalism, small groups fight
a losing battle. Renouvier implored his French colleagues to
become members of small Protestant churches, but he was
not able to save France. James, too, would still belong to the
past only, if he had no message for the armies that must overcome fruitless, sterile work for work's sake, production for
the sake of production, bigness for the sake of bigness. Fortunately he has such a message. In fact, there is in William
James a legacy which is pernicious unless he is seen in his
twentieth century promise. The twentieth century William
James must help us against his admirers styled 19th century.
These admirers know everything about James and ignore
his call to action.

James the lover of the universe, and James the pragmatist
may be misconstrued as the American Spengler and the
American father of Fascism. Mussolini read James, and many
Americans have admired Mussolini. Fascism "works" as the
Nazi victories show. And I see many American liberals falter
and bow in admiration to mental cocktails like Rosenberg's
Myth of the 20th Century and similar pluralistic humbugs,
because James accustomed them to "a pluralistic universe"
and to an impotent, finite God. Polytheism is rampant in
our days, as a consequence of James' resolve, however mis-
understood, to give up logic squarely. Bradley warned James:
"You are going back from Christianity to something lower."
And James Ward wrote: "Your use of the word "consciousness"
seems utter nonsense, and leads to disaster." The masses may be
made conscious of anything; if "consciousness" is man's whole

pride, you can fill man's consciousness with the intent to murder as the Nazis do, and make them feel fine. And James' "Will
to Believe" ushered in the revolt of the masses, because it with-
drew from our faith in God its prop: God's faith in Man.

The masses are plunged into night when the word "faith"
is made dependent on human will, instead of meaning that
God holds us in the palm of his hand. The Greek and Hebrew
word for faith means God's faithfulness and trust. Your
belief and mine is but the poor reflex of God's faithfulness
to all of us together. If God did not keep his promises to
mankind, nobody could talk to anybody else with any hope
of success. Hence, we may admit that a pluralistic universe,
with a finite, object-like God in it, is the American edition of all
the heresies that devour Europe before our eyes. They also
teach that "will to believe" in any kind of God or in many gods,
instead of in the true God who does not trust in one man
or one nation, but in us all, and thereby unites us.

However, the dangerous crest of this wave may soon pass,
because the generation that followed James will correct
his misinterpretation of God. God is not a concept but the
right name; and the whole Bible is nothing but the search for
God's right name. On the other hand, Man is not found
except in his conversation with his brothers. God and Man are
not found as long as we use language about "things," "world,"
"nature," certainly not in laboratory tests. Henry James senior
could not reach the world because he started with God.
William James could not reach God because he started
with things. The third corner, man, of the triangle God-
World-Man, James did reach, but only by "giving up logic
squarely and forever"; in other words, James made a break
between World and Man, but did not make the same break
between the universe and God. The principle, however, is the
same. Neither the right names for God nor the vital dialogues
of Men can be deduced from concepts used for the things
of this world. Concepts cannot be "experienced," words and
names can. Man makes the world work, not pragmatically
for his own ends, but as the faithful servant of some higher

design and purpose, in honor and valor, with the eyes of the soul wide open.

William James owed to his theological father the inexhaustible power of his language, although James did not admit any unshakeable truth, eternally begotten, historically made known once and forever, and applicable daily. He did not admit such truth, only because he knew that theological language was gone for good; his own father's life and work had proved this. From his father's frustration, William James knew of the deadlock of theology from the start. That philosophy was in a similar impasse he was able to learn only through a struggle of forty years. But in the process of learning this he begat in himself two qualities which the new century needs and which must fill our veins if western man shall survive at all. And the mobility of his soul led him to a more and more complete mobilization towards that twofold end.

IV

We are at war today. Please, therefore, face the simple question: what loyalty keeps us here together, in the unselfish company of education? Obviously not theology or a dogma any longer. But neither have we a philosophical system from which the many sciences receive their orientation. So where do we get any common orientation? It is easy to see that our loyalty at this juncture is largely renewed by common danger. The most primitive loyalty rests on the common defense against an enemy. It is not enough to be a thinker or a worker, the two shibboleths of 1776 and 1900. The third secular branch of man's government over the earth is his being a soldier. Philosophy cannot omit from its tenets the phenomenon that man must be ready to die in the war against an enemy. Any philosophy which glosses over your duty or mine to die for a cause is eyewash.

And William James recognized this claim of the soldier to be accepted on his own terms. He worked on a book on the military virtues for two years. He never finished it. But at the same time, he addressed clerks and educators, pacifists and women, so that they might become aware of this quite different mode of life. The soldier, he said, represented the heroic qualities of our soul, the Sunday qualities which alone gave meaning and substance to our week-day routine in work. Our untapped resources of energy, our "second wind" became the most vital problem for all individual or national education in his eyes. He began to see that the cities of Man would not survive unless every citizen was made to act as their founder or refounder. In the face of effeminacy, self-castration, prohibition, he exclaimed: "Fie upon such a cattle yard of a planet." In this spirit, saluting the soldier as an essential element in human nature, he wrote his "Moral Equivalent of War." The Carnegie Foundation for Peace twice declined to reprint it. I don't wonder, for here we enter into a soldier's society—but a soldier's who embraced the heavenly combat and the earthly, both under the one term of war. In making every man a partner of war, James did practical repentance. He restored the solidarity and brotherhood of all Men which his theory left undefended and indefensible.

Only the man who has once done the impossible, who has once moved in the sphere of the infinite risk, can return safely to his city as a law-abiding citizen. James saw the nonsense of an absolute either-or-ness between war and peace. *The more people go to war in peacetime, the fewer people have to go to war in wartime.* The difference of soldier and worker is the difference between mobilization of the whole man and specialization of a part of man. And so James' "Moral Equivalent of War" is the bridge from the 19th to the 20th century, from the millennium of statehood to the millennium of one unified Society. As long as wars were external, between states and nations, philosophers could ignore the essence of war. James made the soldiers' heroism the perpetual and indispensable check on the worker's utilitarianism. In this way, warfare was sublimated from an accidental role in wars between states, to an eternal quality of human society as a whole. He made war a special application of the attitude which makes man man,— *the attitude of conquering the impossible, in freedom from fear.*

V

Desirous to become a citizen of this New Europe, this Western World, I have walked with the spirit of William James during the last nine years. He has been the star of my Americanization. In the Old World I had not known his works. He gave me hope even when I saw him forgotten by his own New England and, alas, his too-New England environment. This environment finally rose to fulfill his will. Young men from Dartmouth and Harvard lifted the ban from William James' alleged impracticality. At the thirtieth anniversary of his death, in founding Camp William James,[2] they made his Moral Equivalent of War work. They realized that total mobilization should prevail, not only in armies or in times of so-called war, but just as much at the domestic front and in times of so-called peace. They believed as our prophet who ominously said: "Until an equivalent discipline is organized, I believe that war must have its way."

In that sentence, he prophesied this war. And he himself embodies his conviction. As early as 1887, one of William James' friends interpreted his portrait to him in this way: "You could not have done a nicer thing for me than sending your picture. It is a head for anything; but if seeing it, I had been asked, 'What manner of man is this?' I should have said, 'A soldier in the larger sense' . . . If you will put shoulder straps on it, most people would take it for a picture of General Sherman."

"A soldier in the larger sense . . ." Yes. As Sherman marched through Georgia, James marched through Victorianism with an increasing determination, because he saw a desert there, spreading under the illusions of a decaying manhood. And so he lifted the martial virtues to a universal plane, blending the militia of the State and the militia of Christ into one.

The future of America is in an impasse because of the cleavage between a pacifist theory and a belligerent actuality.

[2] Camp William James in Tunbridge, Vt. was a voluntary work service camp, first organized in 1940 as an experimental camp within the Civilian Conservation Corps. Professor Rosenstock-Huessy was its principal adviser. The camp was a forerunner of the Peace Corps.

America may remain paralyzed if the Moral Equivalent of War is not used to unify the soul of America. Here is a civilian mind, a lover of peace who discovers war and has the courage to "think" it, for the sake of peace, by showing that war and love of the enemy are not incompatible, but enter a new stage today.

I wish I could be more eloquent now. Let me say this simply, that the worker, thinker, soldier, hit hard at the objects or objectives of their will. They are "natural" types of man. The gentleman and the non-conformist are "social" types. They treat man as a member of a congregation or of a society, and mitigate his ruthlessness by making him regard his neighbor. The soldier's steel also must be tempered by the fire of the soul, if he is to remain the brother of all men. The soldier who today is not a member of the whole of humanity endangers it. No enmity between humans can be allowed to be more than relative, lest a world totally at war perish.

Now, James revealed this secret in his own life. A few days before his death, a friend said to him: "I know of no one more universally beloved. I at least never heard an ill word of you from any one." And as early as 1871, James exclaimed: "In America, a regular advance is possible because each man confides in his brothers." A soldier does not idly speculate on the abstract brotherhood of man: he himself remains a brother, still loved even when he contradicts, fights and resists. A William James who can be loved is not simply James who loves; he sets the example of a new world order.

Today, soldiers must restore the capital of our faith which competitive workers and smug intellectuals have consumed. And William James, who confided in his fellowmen, has ennobled the soldiers' task, to convey, arouse, evoke faith. You, the youth of America, on this January 11, 1942, may have a good conscience, because the most illustrious American thinker, worker, and soldier has pre-lived your total mobilization, and lifted it beyond mere imperial war. He has made your way of life one form of creating, through the martial virtues, the unity of the earth; one way of curing our blind souls so that some great design and purpose for the whole of mankind can be worked out here below, for which we have the honor to be the faithful servant; one way not of talking about the brotherhood of man, but of bringing it about.

"Bring it about," William James would say; it will not come about by education, or by accident, or by progress, or by fate or by any causation and mechanism. The universe in which we move is cleft and plural. You have to fill the gaps between its banks and edges, as thinkers, workers, soldiers. The great traditions of the race—freedom, faith, hope—never exist unless thou insisteth upon them. Make nationalism shrink so that the universe can grow.

And so the soul of William James will converse with us when we, in work, in thought, in battle, bring about a growing universe of free people.

References:

Charles Renouvier, La Fin du Sage, Les derniers Entretiens, rec. par L. Prat, Paris 1930.

Louis Prat, *Charles Renouvier, Philosophe,* Paris 1937.

Thought and Character of William James by Ralph Barton Perry, 1935.

Josiah Royce, *William James and other Essays,* 1911.

William James, *A Pluralistic Universe,* New York, 1928.

New York Herald Tribune, Dec. 27, 1941, p. 2.

Letters of William James, I (1920).

The Literary Remains of the Late Henry James, 1884.

American Youth, 1940, Cambridge.

CHAPTER 3

MODERN MAN'S DISINTEGRATION
AND THE EGYPTIAN KA

Disintegration of the Ego

MODERN MAN'S PERSONALITY IS weakened. Modern man is no longer certain of the sources of personal integrity. We see the adults take flight into their expert knowledge, into their "fields" to find certainty and character and distinction. The modern adult does not like politics or any general confession of faith or the emotional vagueness of a "movement." He concentrates on his profession and he is as good a specialist as he can be. But simply by watching how the word "adult" has spread, we may gain an inkling that the modern "adult" is not too strong as a personality. He is called an "adult" from the evidence of statistics about his biological age. When persons are called "adults," there is a divarication of biological and social maturity. We see the boy and adolescent stay young, brutish, shapeless long beyond the years in which his grandfather took shape as a personality and took his place in society as a citizen, in the congregation as a member.

Shapeless youth and specialized or unemployed adults are losing the path towards "personality." This is coupled with a good deal of confusion about "personality." Many a leading scientist, for example, honestly thinks that he owes his personality to his science. Many white collar men and employees honestly think that only scholars or artists can be personalities. Again and again, I hear the college students protest against the idea that they could aspire to personality. "I am just a human being," they stammer. The moderns prefer to be reduced to Egos, to the I, and that is as far as they will go in their self-identification. The recent trends in psychology have elaborated this desolate state of the Ego. It has been said that the Ego seeks the love of a "thou," and that the Ego is often overruled by the subconscious "it." But though propagated by special schools, like psychoanalysis, the public discussion has not seen fit to face squarely the *question of Ego and person*. There is no general understanding what an individual (an Ego) and a personality are, how they are related to each other, whether they form a necessary sequence, or whether they are mere words.

The Ego is one special aspect of the person, developed since 1600, since Descartes' identification of the mind with the soul. Personalities break down today because of the unbalanced victory of the Cartesian doctrine of man as being the Ego, the mind written with the capital "M" of modern idealism, realism, and pragmatism. It is the thesis of this paper that these three schools of thought and in fact all post-Cartesian philosophy entertain a lopsided view of man, and that the simple fact that you, my dear reader, are good enough to read these lines proves that there is in you another force which is not the Ego, but the "thou." Only because you are a listening "thou," listening as to a command, as much as you are a thinking Ego, can you be a person. He who has not listened cannot think.

All modern thinking about man is based on too narrow a concept of his nature. This can be proven with certainty. The fact that you chose to read this essay must have reasons that transcend your and my Egos. As long as you read this essay you act as a listening "thou," not as if you were an Ego. And as little as you are an Ego when you read this, so little is the author whom you read the Ego to whom you consent to listen. But this question is related to the central one at hand: Can man be a person when he starts with the assumption of his being an Ego? Is it an essential a priori of a person to listen, to read, to respond? Is responsiveness an a priori of personality? As a requisite for personality, it officially does not exist among the moderns. Descartes saw our most personal quality in our power to check, to control, to observe and to doubt responses. These constitute the powers of the mind, in the eyes of the moderns. Is this definition wrong? We say that it is. We say that its propagation desiccates all sources of personality today, that modern man's flight into his special field as an expert observer, etc. is the catastrophe of the machine age by which the only source for personal life is buried.

In order to prove this point we shall use Egyptian source material. It is of help to travel to foreign countries and periods for disentangling ourselves from the accidents of birth and environment. We shall find a world in which Descartes' "mind" did not exist, and in which personalities did live. We shall understand finally why neither ancient Egypt nor modern France covered the whole ground in which the sources of personal life rise. This will caution us against narrowing our concept of a person either in the Cartesian or the primitive direction. Making it more comprehensive than it has been during the last three centuries, we shall be able to tap the sap of life at the very core of the tree again. For modern man is just one branch on the tree of life of humanity, and we must reclaim our connection with the whole.

I

The Ka in Egypt is a sign that is represented by two uplifted hands.[1] It bestows life on the king or individual. One's Ka is the "power behind the throne," the life giving genius. The Ka is mentioned in every inscription. It is the essence that has to be listed as present if the individual is to fulfill his function in this world or in the next.

The interpretation of the exact meaning of Ka, then, is of great importance. There have been two schools of thought. And in examining them we shall see that the differentiation between the "thou" and "I" state of mind offers the key to our understanding.

[1] See our picture No. 1, page 192.

Maspero held that the Ka was the alter ego, a duplication of the individual, himself once more. Erman, the greatest authority, saw in Ka the embodiment of the general supply of living energy; Steindorff saw man's genius.

Now it is a fact that the king's Ka alone is represented in pictures. "The king being a God on earth, has, ever since he is born, the privilege of being united to his Ka. This is not the share of ordinary people; the latter reach union with their Ka after death only." (A. Moret, *Le Nil.* etc., 1926 p. 361 n.l.) The representation of the royal Ka shows a bearded man who carries the shield with the name of king.[2] Ka is intimately connected with the name of the king. The Ka is called in Memphis the product of the "Tongue." The Tongue-God made all the Ka-s. (Erman, *Berliner Sitzungsberichte*, 1911, p. 940). The one Ka unfolds into many Ka-s, representing special qualities of the royal power: his hearing, seeing, perceiving, splendor, glory, spellbinding, longevity, his being Reverend, thriving, may all be listed as individual Ka-s. The list sometimes comprises seven, sometimes twice seven, fourteen, but without any persistency in it. The power of the Ka includes everything that characterizes the influence of the king on earth; all special qualities emanate from the central majesty embodied in the Ka.

In Pyramid text 1653, Atum, the god, creates the first two gods in the following manner: "After having made them, he put his arms around them and these arms contained the Ka, and by doing so he gave them divine existence and permanence." And Atum, in this same text is implored to bestow the Ka on the dead king in the same manner.

So far so good. But modern man could not resist the temptation to modernize this strange concept. Von Bissing (Münchener Akademie 1911, *Versuch einer neuen Erklaerung des kai,* p. 5) by his argumentation does us a real service. Taking modern man's psychology for granted in the old times, his logic comes as a real eye-opener. Von Bissing finds that the plural Ka-s (Kau) may represent the power which comes to the dead from the sacrifices. From our general conception of

---

[2] Our picture No. 2.

the Ka, this is but one more emanation of the Ka. Just as much as old names of persons run: "Re is my Ka," "Ptah is my Ka," so the offerings are the dead man's Ka-s and the effect of the offerings on the person for whom they are given is to restore his original power or life energy. Hence the offerings for the dead enter the field of force called Ka, and may finally be called Kau themselves. But Von Bissing, instead of starting with the royal Ka, starts from these Ka-giving offerings for the dead and sentimentalizes on this. He sees the hieroglyph of the two extended arms, and he concludes that the Ka- hieroglyph signifies the arms of the longing soul that extend themselves towards the offerings. He has been refuted by Kees (Hermann Kees, *Die Jenseitsvorstellungen* etc., Leipzig, 1926, p. 75). But for our purposes his slip is valuable.

His interpretation is perfectly reasonable on the basis of our current subjective psychology which teaches every individual to look into the world from his own self as the center of reasoning, as a mind. To identify the Ka with the arms that man stretches out imploringly, lowers the Ka to the level of human weakness and subjectivity. It would be the very opposite of strength or of the process by which man is given a name for himself by the world. We would then have in early Egypt the idea of the "self-made man" indeed. The Ka would be man pulling himself up by his own boot straps.

Von Bissing is so sure of the universality of his own era's logic that he does not know that this one interpretation is excluded under all circumstances by the Egyptian tradition. The name is always "*given*" to a person, and for instance the vulture-goddess of upper Egypt carries the Ka protectingly over the king's head. Before the Cartesian mentality conquered, man never thought that the mental processes originated in himself. The Ka always is a power that is given to man, not made by him. Shakespeare in Romeo and Juliet has a verse that shows the root of the Ka in the human soul. When Juliet has called Romeo, Shakespeare makes Romeo exclaim: "It is my soul that calls upon my name." To the vulgar psychology this is sheer nonsense. Is the soul then outside of Romeo since he is called from the outside by the name? Vulgar psychology holds that the body of Romeo is here and now first, and that the word Romeo is just a label, a word, by which he may register in documents or statistics.

Modern psychology and logic starts thinking at the aspect of speech as hanging words upon things. Modern logic puts the objective fact of "somebody," first, the social fact of his being labelled Romeo, second, and the fact that other people may define this Romeo comes third. Thus their a priori is the body, and their aposteriori is the label. 1. self, objective Ego. 2. label, concept, classification. 3. use of this classification or label by others. The Egyptian logic and, I suppose, all non-Cartesian logic does just the opposite. It does not even know that man may use the term "The Ego." This term does not occur before 1780. This coupling of the demonstrative article, which points outside into the external world, with the word "I," which always points inside to the living power, the "sacred vigour" of the Homeric kings and the majesty of all those in authority who may speak in their own name, is not even two hundred years old. It is a hybrid formation. The deadlock of modern logic results from the fact that it is not understood as a hybrid and irrational form. "The Ego" is a contradiction in terms.

II. Powerless and Powerful Language

In order to learn from Von Bissing's wrong interpretation of the Ka in Egyptian religion all that modern thinking may learn from it for the evaluation of the Ego concept, we must now ask the reader to enlarge on his assumption that language consists of words. This assumption is too narrow. To say that language is contained in the dictionary is a half truth. The state of language in the dictionary is a special state of affairs. A dictionary is the "reduction" of language to the aggregate state of mere words. "Words" are language which is powerless, which is dismissed or spent. "Words" are spent language waiting for resurrection. As mere words language finds itself between two other phases of its circulatory process, between the use of language for conceptual purposes, for thought, and its use for the other purpose, nearly overlooked, ridiculed as arbitrary: for naming things. This nearly lost distinction between concept or word and name is parallel to the paradox of Ka and Ego. What is the distinction between a word and a name?

The name is the state of speech in which we do not speak of people or things or values, but in which we speak *to* people, things, and values. The words "forget," "me," "not" are three words of the English grammer. However, "Forget-me-Not" is the name with which man addressed this plant. They are the right words for the plant. The right word is that word under which the thing so named will move and obey and come forth and be a part of the realm created by my linguistic influence. When Orpheus invoked the walls of Thebai to go up under the tones of his music, he moved people or stones to do that which he wanted them to do. All perusal of language in the form of names has exactly this intention. To speak of the Congress of Industrial Organizations is to use words. To speak of the CIO, is to speak of it politically, making use of all its associations with feelings of antipathy and sympathy, with emotions and motions. Names today are hidden in letters like AAA, CCC, NYA. I deem this significant for the philosophy of our era.

For centuries our philosophy has been exclusively concerned with words on one hand, and concepts on the other. The social life of language, however, is that of names which have power to move people and things. And since words were denied this quality in our era of reason, the power of names crept back into our lives through the back door of letters which read so similarly to the formulas of chemistry. In chemistry, at least, we all admitted the step from analysis to synthesis, and in chemistry, the analytical formula served the technician to produce, to resuscitate, to commandeer the substance thus labelled. Now, in a carry-over of this scientific process from word ("Oxygen"), to "O" = 16, to recipe ("take two units of O and mix them in such and such a way") we today are recognizing the power of the CIO over millions of people. The CIO is, so to speak, the Ka that gives life, glory, dignity, to unskilled workers all over this country. It is quite obvious that CIO is not a word which they use but a name under which they are addressed and which they recognize as being their address. And "CIO" is the right way of addressing them as far as the CIO is successful.

The name is the right address of a person under which he or she will respond. The original meaning of language was this very fact that it could be used to make people respond. The very word "responsiveness" today is less popular than its often invoked variation—"responsibility." I am responsible for something objective. The complaint is heard often that people are not responsible enough. However, may it not be true that we cannot be responsible when we are not allowed to be responsive first? If no soul calls upon our name, we perhaps are too weak to shoulder responsibilities. As long as we are only taught and addressed in the mass, our name never falls upon us as the power that dresses our wounds, lifts our hearts, and makes us rise and walk.

The right words, i.e. "names," guarantees responsiveness. Responsiveness is the lying open for being empowered. We have long spoken of an open mind. But the mind is open for conceptual understanding of the things outside. The other openness of any human being is to an appeal made to him in the power of his name. "As an American, as a human being, as a Christian, as a believer, as a child of God, you must listen," this appeal might say. "All members of the CIO do so and so," is another form which this appeal may take. We, too, have not just one Ka under which we are moved. The first name, the family name, our professional title as a doctor, or scholar, or a farmer, as a native of this state, a resident of another, may be listed as so many kas which bestow on us responsiveness.

Now, the power of a name lies in the fact that it eases our conscience. The simple fact, that the mother calls the child by the right name, makes the child smile. The cry, which is the first utterance of the child when it enters the world, is transformed into the smile of response through the intermediary of the name. The name pacifies the child and gives it ease in this new and cold world which it did not enjoy before. *Names give orientation.* As long as we are addressed with a name that has power we feel that we are led. We may smile, because, even when an enemy calls our name, we still are not confused. We know where we are. In as far as our society is imperilled today it is because people are not addressed in the powerful manner which might give them orientation.

All religion tried to give orientation. All religion is out for the right word in the right place and time. All superstitions arose because religions wanted eternal recipes for giving names. The true life of human speech defies all recipes. The names under which the parts of the world must be made to move change with the times. But that does not mean that the appeal must not be made. The fact that no one name lasts forever in its power over an open heart only means that our minds do transform constantly powerful names into mere words and concepts. And once a word is definitely analyzed and conceptualised, it has lost its quality of name. Any definition cuts the umbilical cord between the use of an element of speech as a name and the use of the same element as a mere word.

Because we need orientation, we wait for our soul to call upon our name. This fact leads to one other difference between words and name. All words can be used by everybody and can be carried over to any number of things and objects either by definition or metaphorically. But the same element of speech when used as a name is neither a metaphor nor a classification. It is exclusively used between you and me. If the child was not sure that the mother meant him, Johnny, only, and nobody else, the child would not smile. The name is personal, or it is no name. Personifications are possible only as long as language is name-giving. Because name is personification. The word is generic, the name is specific.[3] Names are exclusive speech between a person and somebody whom he tries to make into a person by calling him with the right

[3] This is essential for the solution of the dispute over the "universalia." It cannot be understood without dealing with the "names" of God.

name. Whereas a description of the outer world may be given in words, the orientation of you or me in the world can only be given us by a specific name-giving process to which we then respond. Orientation and response are two aspects of one and the same process. The child which hears itself called by the same name again and again, responds and thereby gains orientation.

"Orientation" is the objective aspect and "response" is the subjective aspect of one and the same social process of giving or using the right name.

Words classify, but names orient. Words generalize, but names personify. Words dismiss living subjects into the realm of objectivity. Names pick up the little baby or the flower or the sun, and incorporate them into one society of communication. Without names, communication would be impossible. For before two individuals may talk to each other in words about things, they must be mutually responsive, they must recognize each other as persons. Each must make more and more of a person out of his interlocutor by giving each other names. Even abusive name-calling is better than nothing. Because, although negative reaction, it is a condition for the person in the individual who is "called names."

Our present-day discussions about communication usually stress the Babylonian confusion in terminology. As many people, as many definitions of democracy. But communication will not improve on the objective front of definitions as long as we do not make sure in whose name we speak to each other. Whose name do we carry when we speak to each other about the weather, or about the true, the beautiful and the good? The great problem of our days is whether man speaks to man anonymously or only as an incognito slowly to become known as a person. Communication can take place between people who are eager to personify their interlocutor more and more. Communication dies down between people who wish to remain anonymous to each other forever.

The linguistic elements in their name-giving phase are the "word" with a capital W; as words they are mere words, and used in vain. As concepts, they are purified and wait for their resurrection. And this constant process from name to word to concept to name again, is the life of the Word. Whenever any one phase is omitted, society disintegrates because its members lose orientation.

III. Orientation in Egypt

The Egyptian Ka oriented the King. It authorized him to govern in wisdom, knowledge, in right perception and insight, glory permanence, as Horus, the reborn son of the ever dying, ever resurrecting Osiris. It is not difficult to trace the development of the Ka from the gods to the king and only much later to the individual Egyptian for his life after death. Without pretending to say the final word here, we may however mention some indisputable facts.

Before the Nile and its inundations created the unity of work and law in Egypt, the life in Egypt did not differ from that in the Libyan oasis and other parts of Africa.[4] The chieftain of any tribe, in this hot climate, was responsible for the rainfall. And he gave way to a successor every seventh or ninth year because the magical power of rain-making had to be regenerated regularly.

When Osiris discovered the possibilities of the Nile valley, and the regular flow of the fertile mud between July and October, the Egyptians gave up the universal fear of primitive men against the low land of the valleys, and closed the new "city" ("nwt") of Egypt against Northerners, Westerners, Easterners and Southerners,[5] rejected the God of Libya, Seth, and turned their new temples to the service of the two gods that did not simply represent the unruly wind, rain, and clouds of the sky—as Seth—but who did represent the unbroken order of this sky as horizon and sun, Horus and Ra.

The sun, a curse in this hot climate so far, now became a blessing because "he" could set a unified law and order for

[4] Wainwright, G. A., *The Sky-Religion in Egypt*, p. 8 ff., 1938, Cambridge.
[5] James H. Breasted, *Development of Religion and Thought in Egypt*, New York, 1912, pp. 13 and 14.

the thousands of miles of Egypt's length. The pyramid stone
on the obelisk in Heliopolis became "the great occasion for
chaining a cosmic power to a definite and specific place of
worship."[6] Here, the sun cut out a definite place, a temple
on earth that reflected the recurrent order of the sky. A temple is the mirror of heaven. As long as the sky god Seth
governed, no "temple," but altars only, had been possible.
The Egyptian temple reflects eternity.[7] The chieftain of old,
the rain sorcerer, now became the owner of the magical mirror
of heaven on earth. The Pharaoh was not a king in our modern sense of the word. He was the owner of the first revealing
and sacred house of man on earth, of the "city of Egypt"
given by the gods to man in the sacred order of the year that
from eternity to eternity guaranteed the fertility of the land
through the inundation of the Nile. The word Nile now became the word for rain, too. And instead of seven or nine
years of government, Pharaoh shared the eternity of the celestial orders. When he built his pyramid in imitation of the
benben stone in On (Heliopolis), he thereby became the
undying Sun-god himself, Ra.

So Pharaoh was lifted up from a rain sorcerer of Libyan
days, to the steward of God's house on earth, the Sun God.
The sun was lifted every morning by the god Nun up to
heaven with two outstretched arms.[8] We find pictures showing the God lifting the fiery ball over his head.[9] Then we find
two outstretched arms based on the two signs for eternity
("ded"), and life, and again these arms throw up the ball of
the sun.[10] In other pictures the celestial god reaches out with
his two arms for the sun, when the night gives way to the
morning.[11] The gesture of the two arms that lift up the sun
every morning signalizes the central problem of the new faith
that was the "Constitution" of Egypt. Now, if the sun, Ra,

[6] Herman Kees, *Totenglauben und Jenseitsvorstellungen der alten Agyp-ter* Leipzig. 1926, p. 35.
[7] Kees, p. 7.
[8] Kurt Sethe, *Altagyptische Vorstellungen vom Lauf der Sonne*, Preus-sische Akademie der Wiss., phil.-hist. Klasse, SB, 1928, 259 ff.
[9] Sethe, p. 262, our picture no. 3.
[10] Sethe, 271 f, our picture no. 4.
[11] Sethe, 268 and 276.

the model of every Pharaoh, had to be lifted by the god of the source waters up to the horizon every morning, Pharaoh too had to be lifted up to his throne by the Ka.

On the other hand, the individual Egyptian had nothing to do with the sun in the beginning except to worship "him" —certainly he could not think of identifying his own life on earth with that of Ra. It took fifteen hundred years before every Egyptian saw his own life finally end in an atonement with the course and orbit of the Sun in after life. His first great model of the eternal, undying, recurrent life, with "*ded*," permanency, in the houses of "millions of years," as the temples were called,[12] was not Horus, the god of the celestial horizon, or Ra, the sun, directly; his model was his king who, by entering the City of Egypt, the "settlements made in the name of Horus,"[13] had been lifted from a mere chieftain and medicine man into the Pharaoh, the surveyor[13a] of the divine house that reflected heaven on earth and forced heaven down to earth. The King's Ka or majesty consisted in the fact that his raiment no longer was a barbaric tattoo or mask, but the cosmic house and temple itself. The King of Egypt was the first human being who dropped all tribal masquerading and went clean shaven, unmasked and untattooed. For this king had donned the garment of celestial order. It is too weak a word to say that Pharaoh "inhabited" the cosmic gates. His whole life was transplanted upon the celestial wheels, and followed the cosmic calendar hourly and daily and annually in the house.

The Egyptian king was the link between heaven and earth, and in the king's "*name*" the forces of the cosmos and the recognition by society coincided. The radiations of the Ka range from alimentation to glory. But this, though it has puzzled many an Egyptologist,[14] will always result from a happy intersection of the cosmic and the social. We all crave for a necessary role in nature to be recognized by society. We

[12] A. Moret, *Le Nil et La Civilisation Egyptienne*, 1926, p. 148.
[13] Breasted, p. 14.
[13a] Pharaoh surveyed the orientation of every temple.
[14] See especially von Bissing, p. 1 ff. and Moret's famous book of 1902.

all wish to yield a reasonable, necessary and, that is, natural function under the official sanction of society. The doctor can function as a force in nature only through the power which he wields over real processes of life and death: he operates, feeds, and treats and these are real interventions with the cosmos. On the other hand, he is called a doctor, hands out prescriptions which go to the pharmacist, and talks to the patient's family and nurse, and all these are social processes of being named and recognized by organized society. In the same manner, the Pharaoh who reconciles Egypt with the life of heaven, who is lifted up by eternal alimentation to the millions of years of the stature of the Sun, is lifted up before his people by his name and authority and glory. Both cosmic reality and social recognition are two aspects of one and the same thing. We all crave for this unity between our cosmic and our social role. No wonder, then, that both are covered by the gesture, the process, the divine event which is called "ka."

In Abydos, Pharaoh Seti the First sits before his table of offerings; behind him, his "ka" walks as a bearded man, carrying on his head the Ka-sign, the two uplifted arms with the name of the God-King "Horus Ra." That is, the name by which he is lifted up to the millions of years of the run of the celestial orb. Besides, the Ka-carrier has in his right hand the sign of eternal life, and in the left arm he lifts a pole like the one on which the Romans carried their eagles. But, instead of the eagle, the ka sign is on this pole. Above the hieroglyph for the god-king and inside the two outstretched arms of the ka sign balances the sign "sa," protection. To be lifted up as the sun rises every morning, means to be protected, to have both a necessary role in the cosmos and an established name in society. To have one's ka—who would not wish that his nature and his society could agree in so perfect harmony as the Ka of Pharaoh?

The Ka was held up above the king so that he might feel that he only had to respond. Names unburden our soul immeasurably from our own choices. They tell us what our destiny is. The Egyptian ka is an eternal category because it unifies the meaning of the name and of the orientation of a person. Persons are oriented individuals.

IV. Disintegration and Orientation

A person is not an individual that can think. But a person is an individual whose soul has called upon his name and thereby determined the direction of his life. A person is a man who has been given direction. When a scientist follows his logical analysis, his laboratory experiments, his die is cast. He has responded to the direction of his life; he has acknowledged the imperative written over his own life: there shall be science and you shall be the servant of science. Nothing that this scientist thinks or writes or publishes within his scientific field makes sense outside this decision that he had made long before. He responded to the call of science long before he knew what he would do during his life as a scientist. He got his orientation by moving along on the wave length that had appealed to him when he dialed his reception apparatus. Descartes is the founder of modern science because he made a decision in 1620 that his life would be oriented solely by the idea of a progressive scientific research program. You do not share the answer given by Descartes, the scientist, but you share the response given by Descartes, the man.

The response to science precedes any scientific statement in particular. Man is called upon by other vocations of a non-scientific character just as well. And any science of society must penetrate behind the decision made by the scientist, must see that the scientist is not the normal type of human being but just one among others, in order to discover the essential composition of the good society. The notion of persons in a society and the notion of scientists must never be allowed to coincide. The orientation of an individual that makes him become President or scientist or baker is a decision that makes president and scientist and baker equals as responsive and oriented persons long before their various ideals of presidency, scholarship, and bakership begin to operate upon them. The democracy of a scientific age can only be retained and saved when the scientist willingly remains a part of the people in this democracy. How can this be done? The scientist must hold to the faith that every person that decides to become a scientist does so not as a scientist but as a human being who harkens to his deepest calling. Then he will realize that his own decision unites him with all people who grow into responsive, named, oriented persons. The scientist is a personality as a member of humanity, not as a member of the academic class.

The Egyptian world, literally in the childhood of humanity, explored the one and uppermost experience of the child's mind: that of being addressed, of having been loved and called upon and directed by elders who did not run away as animals do when they have fed their fledglings, but who stood by the young, the children, the grandchildren, the great and great-great grandchildren forever. The Ka, the name-giving character of speech became the aspect of all logical processes that was realized and revered and fructified to the extreme.

Our era has suppressed the very notion of this mental situation. Descartes complained that for twenty years his brain had been corrupted by confused and wrong notions. He complained that Descartes the man had been anteceded by Descartes the child. The confidence between his father's religion and his own science was destroyed. He thought that the name-giving relations in society were sheer waste. He and his followers have destroyed the cement that connects the living bricks of our social temple, called persons. This cement is the right name. Neither Descartes nor Egypt are wholly right. The name which a man is given binds him to two achievements equally difficult: to go forward as a specialist and to remain a human being as the perfect men before him. The essence of the era in which we live is that man as a specialist shall progress and have an open mind. But this era will end in catastrophe if it forgets that, as a human being, man must have the same open heart that made the first fully human being the heart of the world. The mind listens to words for objects; the heart listens for its clue for personal orientation, its proper name on the stage of history. The open mind that understands words and the responsive heart that is called by its name represent the polarity of human mentality which we must uphold.

The Ego and the Ka are both real sources of our personal life. We now can form certain conclusions from the fact that the Ego who uses words to manipulate things and the Ka that calls me by my name to move me, have opposite principles of political economy. When I use words, I always try to get a maximum result with a minimum effort. If I can say something in three lines, I shall not waste four paragraphs. He would be a fool who would waste his energy on a task for which he need not spend more than five minutes with the right tools.

Do as much as you can with as little effort as possible, is the motto of the anonymous, impersonal, objective, scientific mind. This Cartesian mind has successfully discovered how to use fewer and fewer means for bigger and bigger results. A modern factory is the ideal display of this economizing in words, in organization. This economy, however, cannot apply to man himself. He must still find some incentive for an "all-out" attitude. Man must still feel called forth as being good for something. He would be a rascal who, out of sheer indolence, would not use his full energy. Cartesian logic reduces man's responses to minimum responses. For every individual or particular task this reductionism is valuable. But when it means that these savings in time or effort reduce man's stature, when it means that because I only have to work three hours for my daily bread in the future, I also will only be fully alive three hours of my day, then the person is thwarted. For a person is a man who responds with his whole heart to his calling. And any element of the universe that whispers to a human being, "respond lest I die," calls forth this man personally to his human destiny. "All out" is the attitude of the man who has heard his calling and who knows that he can only become a person in the process of responding to his calling. Man must be both indolent and all out. When his mind can find a shorter way, a better tool, he may save energy. The mind is our saver of energy; this is what we call the Ego.

But the soul is our investor, our spendthrift, our saviour when life seems to die from inertia and indifference and lack of orientation.

The "thou" is not a figure of speech, but a corollary to the "Ego." When the concept of the Ka in Egypt hardened and when the concept of the Ego as conceived by Descartes became the only motor in the life of the mind, then both obstruct the mental process. Egypt went fossil because Ka, name, was every word. No name could die. Our society disintegrates because no name is allowed to authorize and to call forth persons. The Ka of Egypt and the mind of Descartes each alone obstruct the constant flow of creative speech through individuals that must guarantee the orientation of society.

CHAPTER 4

THE FOUR PHASES OF SPEECH

Introductory Note

DR. RICHARD KOCH AND Eugen Rosenstock-Huessy had, in 1922–23, studied Paracelsus together in Germany. Koch taught medicine at the University of Frankfurt and was Franz Rosenzweig's doctor. He fled Nazi Germany in 1937, went to Russia and worked as a physician in Essentuki on the Black Sea. After the Second World War Koch in Russia and Rosenstock-Huessy in the United States wrote to each other again.

Koch wrote to Rosenstock-Huessy because he, now a brain specialist, believed he had discovered in the "lamina quadrigemina" in the human brain an organ which acts as the seat of the great impulses of the species. Here the impact of what our senses register, and what others say to us, here our profoundest insights, Koch says, are recorded. The individual cortex then acts as a brake to the total reaction which is received in the "lamina quadrigemina." The cortex, so to speak, cuts this total impact into pieces. The "lamina quadrigemina" is situated between the spinal cord and the cortex. All vertebrates have this organ in common. So far not much has been known about it, however it has been considered to be an archaic organ.

Koch wanted to tell Rosenstock-Huessy that the "lamina quadrigemina" might furnish the anatomical proof for Buber's, Rosenzweig's and Rosenstock-Huessy's insights into human speech. The speaker, they say, never speaks as an individual only, but always for the species.

Koch was scheduled to report his findings to the Institute

for Neurology at the Academy of Medical Science in Moscow. He died from heart failure before this could take place, shortly after his last letter to Eugen Rosenstock-Huessy in 1947.

A Letter to Richard Koch, Essentuki, Russia

Nov. 4, 1947

Dear Friend:

After my long letter to you I came in the lecture room upon the same complex of questions. In telling the students of your Quadrigemina Theory, I continued the conversation with you.

You say that the blocks of the cortex prevent an invasion of our pictures of the world by a total reaction. Vice versa, it is equally true that speech saves the totality of experience in the midst of the blocks and channelizes it through these blocks.

Speech is, in fact, the means by which a total experience penetrates in an orderly fashion into the departments of conscious life. If I understand you, your analysis of the brain starts from the fact that the brain is meant to prevent a short circuit in the form of an explosive total reaction to a total experience. I start from the creative aspect of this impediment. Something is achieved by this system of brakes and this something is nothing less than the social digestion of any experience made by one member of the human family. If one "individual" could and would "react" to his own experiences fully and get them "out of his system" by himself, man would not be man. We always experience as specimens of the species. Our experiences enter the whole of society because we have not experienced before we have responded as specimens of the species. The total reaction is blocked up in order to force communication upon the member of the human family who is out in front.

What then is the difference between individual and specimen? The specimen is seed and fruit. Whenever we experience totally, on faith, the species represented by us experiences. And these experiences acquire new faculties. Speech is the way of transmitting acquired faculties. There is no other. It is a way, as I need not underline to you, which is *material*. To speak does something very powerful to the realm of matter. Sounds have energy.

The articulation of a new experience can be compared to the refraction of light in a prism. The spectrum of colors contains yellow, blue, red, etc. although they all reflect "light." For our analogy yellow, blue, red are the great fundamental persons of grammar: politics, art, law, science; thou, I, we, it. And "faith" is the believed-in unity of the total experience while it undergoes its diffusion or articulation in the brain's departments.

Light and colors cannot be separated. In the same manner faith and the forms of speech cannot be separated. The forms of speech are the articulation of one act of faith into its worldly acts of penetration and communication and naturalization.

Human speech never was intended for expressing platitudes like "the weather is bad," or "come," or "I am happy," or "the moon rises." Human speech corresponds to the construction of our brain so as to permit the transfer of acquired experiences to the race. Speech enables us to gain times and spaces for "settling" a question. Speech *connects* the departments of experience. The event which is expressed can only be expressed in four phases. And the event has not happened, has not eventuated at all unless it has mobilized all the four phasic responses. Not only must the experience pass through these four distinguishable phases, aspects or modes, but also the sequence of these modes is fixed. And the cunning of individuals in omitting one phase or the other is doomed to failure. Our whole civilization tries to omit one phase or the other and is for that reason doomed to failure. Speech holds on to the proper order by its rules of grammar.

The four phases of speech may be distinguished as follows:

1. *Fiativum*   (political event)
2. *Subjectivum*   (art and literature)
3. *Perfectum*   (legislation)
4. *Abstractum*   (objects in nature)

The terms are chosen to show the polarity of 1 and 3, 2 and 4. They also could be grouped around the specific eccentricity shown by the specimen in each phase. For the experiencing specimen is 1. *prejected* in the *fiativum* into the unknown. He is 2. *subjected* to the uncertainties of suspense while he sighs, sings, swears and undergoes the pressures of the agenda in process. He 3. is *trajected* over the river of time whenever he can report back "order fulfilled": we have done it. He 4. is *object* of his own analysis after it is all over and he has been dismissed from the exigencies of the situation. Then the object, the event, is a mere "it."

1. Preject
2. Subject
3. Traject
4. Object

everybody experiences when he:

1. Falls in love prejectedly: Love me!
2. Courts and is lyrical—subjectively.
3. Stands at the altar: we have done it, we have come across.
4. Introduces her to the first stranger as "my wife," objectively.

In a closer analysis of the four phases, many more serious processes receive their place. First, the "Harken Israel," the event which means you and nobody else, destines and singles out. The famous principle of selection of Darwin occurs right now and here whenever one specimen listens. For if he listens in the full sense of the term, then the "thou" which listens comprises his genitals, heart, brain and hands and stomach, altogether.

Second, the *subjectivum* creates the social, mental or intellectual group which is introduced to the event together with the first person who is struck by the lightning. Subjective submission to an event leads to lyrical utterance which is always democratic. A man who sings his heart out imparts this heart-subjectivity to all his equals. This democratisation of an experience enabled Moses to impart his listening to God to all Israel. It enabled Goethe to impart his conquest of suicide in his Werther to innumerable readers. That experience is intended to be personal plus common is shown by the polarity of any *fiativum* which befalls one—the hero of this issue or event—and the *subjectivum* which gives him comrades for the experience.

The "mind" accomplishes this democratic moulding of a dictatorial experience. The first person which moulds the mind is always subjective. The hero never is: he is prejective because he is made over into a new realm of experience and has not yet any "feelings"; hence the hero is "thou"; to himself the hero appears as the instrument of God, as the servant of the word, as the ear of a mouth. The "and God spake to Moses" simply is the correct observation of Moses' plastic situation. In Deuteronomy we have the same Moses' subjective song depicting his "mind."

In the same book, we have his laws, which are the event when it is reported. This is the third phase, the *perfectum*. The subjective pressure of a deep emotion is transformed into the narrative of a past whenever the hero's "thou" and the subject's "I" can be tranquillized into a "we." Lindberg called the book about his transatlantic flight We in a most felicitous phrase, as it told the tale of his plane and himself, and tales require some "we."

From this we can see that the grammatical form of the "indicative" is at home in the perfect and the past. The future has the imperative and the present has the subjective forms which we call optatives and subjunctives, as indispensable modes of their very existence. Neither the future nor the present is in need of a form of speech in the indicative. However, "we have flown to Paris" cannot be expressed in any other way than by the statement of fact. "We got married" is therefore a more primeval form of speech than "I run," "I go." In fact, the long "o" of Latin in *amo* (I love) is clearly subjective and shows that the alleged indicative of the present for the first person is a mere borrowing from the originally unique form of any "I," the subjunctive of suspense.

Thus, the tale of an event is the tail light of the event. Nothing has happened which is not reported back as having happened. History is not arbitrary staring at bygone things. History is the articulation of the event itself in its participants; as the event goes by, it proves its passing by being told as a tale. The historian certainly is not the onlooker of an event but the last man whom the event produces. Or in the man who does and tells, the tale which he tells of his hunt is necessary to the restoration of his own freedom from the event. Psychoanalysis allows people to tell the end of their tales because the fixation of the *fiativum* can only cease by transforming the patient's *fiativum* and *subjectivum* into his *perfectum*, his tell tale stage. Of course, the psychoanalytic mode of expression is superfluous in all the positive circuits of speech where the *fiat* is not abortive but succeeded by the communicative lyrical and the statutory historical modes of speech.

These three phases of speech—dramatics, lyrics, epics—have been known to all men always as indispensable and as normal. The fourth phase, analytics, is indispensable too, but the men of antiquity denied that it was *normal*. On the other hand, our times have declared that the first three phases were dispensable, and that the fourth phase was both normal and imperative.

The analytical phase of speech is the *abstractum* as opposed to the *subjectivum*. In this phase the movement dies and is discarded as merely natural. "Nature" we call everything which exists without "you," without "me" and without "us." Or more correctly, "natural" is any experience in as far as we look at it as though it had nothing to do with us. When we tell a criminal that his act was only natural, he is relieved. For we tell him that he is not responsible for it, that he need not waste any feelings about it and that he need not report it to the police. Now these three things precisely constituted his crime before it became natural: his selection for this villainy was his heroic dramatization. His qualms of conscience were his *subjectivum*, and his relation to the law was the historical place achieved for his act.

In the "natural," the act is dismissed. "Nature" laughs at God's "let there be light" as it is the attitude which cannot say anything except "there is light." The fourth phase of speech is the spirit's death. If we call the impetus by which a total experience subjects one man to the four phases through which the experience is realized "spirit," i.e., a breath of life, then phase four is the phase in which the spirit dies but the specimen recovers. If phase four did not abstract us from our spells, freedom could not exist to start a new phase. In phase four we expire one act of faith so that we may be inspired again. In literature our times have created the analytical novel, the naturalistic picture of an event. This is neither drama nor lyrics nor epics; it is scientific prose. Of course it has never flourished before, as only we have made a cult of the abstract, of phase four. We have inserted death into all cycles of inspiration. Generalisations have become our gods. They are abstract. Great liberty has thus been achieved. But the deification of the abstract is impossible. Speech remains speech, and its cycle still requires obedience. To say "light is waves," seems to too many to replace the other three forms of truth:

1. "Let there be light."
2. "Let us praise the light."
3. "The sun has risen."

After these three, no. 4, "light is waves" is in order.

The appropriation of an experience cannot succeed in any other order than in the order of *fiativum, subjectivum, perfectum, abstractum.* Thy soul, my mind, our statute and its nature, all color any event. After they all have colored it, it has a place in time and space. And that means it is known as a necessary, digested, transmitted experience of the human race.

All things which are introduced as ideas or as facts to us remain playthings. The only open sesame to an historical experience is a specimen's love for it to such a degree that he will be ready to die for it. Idealists and materialists are irrelevant to history. Love alone can incarnate any new experience into our bloodstreams. A specimen who dies in battle impregnates the species with specific qualities, with the qualities with which he is in love and which he defends or propagates. A specimen is not an individual but the fruit of the specific tree of mankind which holds power over both his individual and his genital elements in turn. The historical specimen—in contrast to the abstract natural individual—experiences an event alternatingly by his propagatory and his individual organs. An incorrect method of experience leads to a castration complex which proves that the experience affects the species-organs directly.

The "quadrigemina" or four phase process of grammatical and articulated speech seems to alternate between the sexual and the individual organs of the specimen in making its appeals. But there can be no doubt that speech begins with an appeal to the species and the specimen's membership in the species, because all speech disarms and invites the putting down of the speaker's physiological defenses. A man is taken outside himself by his voice and invites those who listen to accompany him on this ride into the new environment which his speech delineates.

All speech rides the future of a new heaven and a new earth. All speech draws out the speaker from behind his isolation into a realm of communality with the person or persons who listen. This realm is not a mere fantasy; some material partition in space and some historical bridge through time must result from speech when it is in full force.

These facts require a more detailed consideration. To prepare for an understanding that all articulate speech articulates changing spaces and distinguishes changing periods, please observe that you experience time in a manner directly opposite from space. It is mere indolence which compares space and time as by and large parallel frames of reference. They come to us as extremes on opposite poles. Space is at the start universal, comprehensive, one. Time is at the start momentary, split, atomized, many seconds. We always begin by experiencing innumerable times and one space. And we try desperately to reduce the number of disconnected moments and to increase the number of subdivisions in space! Each home, each nation is intruded into the world of space as an afterthought. Property is a dividing line driven into space with absolute propriety because we consider all space as a task for partitions, walls, boundaries and limitations.

The opposite is true of time. In time we all crave growing units of hours, days, weeks, years, centuries, eras. One single history, however, seems utopian to this very day. But it is of the greatest practical concern to us at this moment. For only the community of One Time and One History may now be possible. Any shorter aspect of the times has become suicidal. But any aspect of the times which exceeds this second seems purely arbitrary and a mere convention to the "natural" mind. So epoch and periods merely "exist." Today's historians discount them by ways of abstraction.

We say, against such "historians," that the only purpose of all speech has been to make an epoch and to make the new epoch stick. The time-building power of speech is the first cause for speech. The space-dividing power of speech is its second cause. The time-building power always aims at the species. The specimen speaks himself and his listeners into a new type of species by taking on a new name, as American or Indian or Christian. The space-building power always aims at the individuals. Which then are the two greatest achievements of the human spirit? If we are right, then the greatest achievements would be the smallest space partition and the most gigantic time bridge.

This is literally true. Any marriage is the whole story of Christ and his Church. The new Testament says, where two or three individuals are gathered in his name, the whole spirit of mankind is alive and present and condensed! How frail this cell is! Vice versa, from Adam to the end of the world stretches a line of continuity which is terribly shaky and delicate and often seems to fall out of our hands into the abyss of time. Whole nations and whole continents leave this continuum and lapse into barbarism. But for this very reason one history for all men is the greatest act of mastery over time. One history for all is not a coarse and crude but a delicate achievement, as delicate as a full communion of heart and soul between two or three in one room's secrecy or privacy.

Why is that so? The smaller my home, the more do I depend for my property on every other man's good will. It is easy for the U.S. to be left alone. But the Swiss are integrated into the whole world for their few square miles of land. Palestine depends on everybody else for its becoming a Jewish homestead.

The German invasion took your Caucasian home. But now turn to the time in which you believe as a doctor and anatomist. This time is measured in terms of progress. As an anatomist of the brain you build on so many past achievements; ergo, you operate there within a time continuum which you deliberately support and expand. Therefore "space" and "time" never are the frame of reference within which we make experiences but they are themselves the phases of realization in our experience. Because in the *fiativum*, the projection into a new situation, we are lassooed into a time corral. What else is the whole history of Israel but the remaining spellbound under the one "Harken Israel" over 3500 years? As soon as a man gives time, heeds any message or any confession, he creates a tension over many seconds of time, he *extends* his faith in this *fiat* into all the moments which it takes to carry out the mission. The *fiativum* creates extended times. Just in doing this and holding the club of an order to be fulfilled over my head the *fiativum* is responded to by me with the *subjectivum*. In this I challenge space to give me a place in which my will to carry out the order may take place and take root. Sentiment requires room around itself, the poet says.

But why is the *fiativum* the true revelation of time, the *subjectivum* the true realization of space? Both lead the individual beyond himself into the species and the society, that is into his conquest of his true time chains and real space contacts. Every powerful name takes me outside my own physical isolation and makes me the bearer of a significant message for the species. Speech conquers death.

Men are meant to speak so that the human race may be like the Single Specimen walking the earth through the ages. Speech is our victory over individual death. It does not abolish death but it triumphs over it. The four phases by which experience enters a man are, then, not meant for his private enjoyment but for his historical service as the cell of one body politic through the ages.

Thus all happening begins as religious order to love unto death; it passes on to intellectual ideal; it becomes a historical act; and it goes out of our system as a natural fact. The four styles or aspects are elements of the event's taking place. The articulation of a total experience to the specimen is religious, idealistic, historical, natural in this order, so that it may come into existence at all.

But this is one side of the whole process only. While the experience comes into existence and "takes place," we ourselves create the place in time and space for this event. And we do this by transforming our previous notions of time and space. No event can take place unless we make room for it. And this entails a radical reorganization of our own time as well as space. Hence, the grammar of experience may open our eyes to what we really mean by these abstract terms "time" and "space."

The inexplicable laziness of the idealists has thrown around these terms "time" and "space" as though any human being ever had experienced time or space in the singular. Nobody ever has. We know of times and spaces. And we know of them under the strict condition that we create and support and believe in at least two spaces and two times simultaneously. We know of time only in the form of twofold time—we distinguish before and after, and we know of space only in the form of duplicate space—we distinguish inner and outer. These four units, two times and two spaces, are the four phases of the total experience. In order to know of them and to master them our faith must drag us through all four of them and must keep us going while in any of the four. Hence, all men always have known of their quadrigeminal existence, as otherwise grammar's dramatic cycles of "go, let us go, we have gone, going," this unity in diversity, could never have been created.

Man connects the duplicate times and the duplicate spaces through which experience takes the whole man and speaks to him as Thou, I, we, he, alternatingly. But it is the whole man, not the individual, who lives through the phases of grammar. It is the child, the son, the lover, the father in us, that is to say our genitals, our heart, our stomach, our hands, all four become representative of the experience in turn. This is no empty phrase but literally true. A man's genitals are eloquent whenever a man dies for a cause. For he then prefers the death of his individuality to the extirpation of the species in the form he himself as a specimen wants it to have.

Idealism has turned the truth topsy-turvy. Idealism starts with one tiny space called the atom and one immense time aspect called infinity. What idealism considers is only the fourth stage of our experiences, the abstract situation in which we dump one certain order, dismiss it from our conscious support into our merely latent "understanding" as a by now naturalized fact. Nature is our space for historical corpses. Natural science expedites historical funerals. Science allows us to start from scratch. It restores the universe and the split second so that we may build new partitions and new time spans.

Grammar, times and spaces, social history, science, religion, illuminate each other. Politics, the arts, law, science are, in this order, thou, I, we, he, written large. Religions attempt to insure the circulation of the living men through all the four phases.

Society is not much interested in the details of political movements, the arts, law, or the sciences. It is vitally interested in their interplay. He who denies the interplay is society's enemy number one! The *health* of society is "diagnosable" by the intimate circulation from person thou, to person I, to person we, to person he, and by a wholesome respect for the sequence thou, I, we, he as inexorable.

CHAPTER 5

THE QUADRILATERAL
OF HUMAN LOGIC[1]

Cogito, ergo sum;   mensuror, quia existo;
audio, ut fiam;   respondeo, etsi mutabor.[2]

THE CARTESIAN REVIVAL OF the Aristotelian tradition is useless
for those processes of thought which do not deal with objects
only, but with ourselves. Their limitation to the two logical
links of "therefore" (*ergo*) and "because" (*quia*) restricts their
usefulness to the classes of either subject or object.

No connection between subjects can ever be explained on
these premises. By a logical self-betrayal, thinkers have spoken
of a *res cogitans,* a thinking thing, for man. But between an
object thought and a listener, no bridge can be established.
The phrase *res cogitans* is a pious lie. By definition, things are
the objects spoken of, never are they spoken to without ceasing
to be *res,* or object. Any transition from "thing" to "listener"
or "speaker" is unwarranted and impermissible. That I weigh
150 pounds and that I can be weighed in for this amount is
totally unrelated to the verity that I may speak, in the least
propitious moment.

It is, however, this pious lie which has enabled the rationalist to pose as a thinker during the last 300 years; for the pre-

[1] A paper contributed by Rosenstock-Huessy to a symposium on his
thought held at the Center for the Study of Religion and Social Issues,
Woods Hole, Mass., 1965.
[2] I think, therefore I am; I will be measured because I exist; I hear
so that I may come to exist; I respond although I will be changed.

ceding 1500 years, it always was admitted that the two classes of objects and subjects are quite insufficient to cope with any serious question of life and death. Dead things, Cartesius could try to understand, and the mentality needed for their understanding he could define. His relations to his Dutch sweetheart and their illegitimate child were quite outside the Cartesian world of understanding. He only underwent them, but did not understand them.

Since, however, even today the average layman is a Cartesian, I have explicitly added two more guiding sentences on those statements which have nothing to do with a subject or an object but which concern us as fellows of other men. And the thought processes and statements which prevail between people are obviously divided into those by which I am told by others who can demand that I listen to them and into those by which I am entitled to tell others what I think of them.

The "Harken, Israel" is the most general command or description of our duty to listen to others. And I have only reworded it in a concession to the egocentric Cartesian formula, by writing: *audio ut fiam* in the place of "Harken, thou man." To be called by his true name is part of any listener's process of becoming his true self. We have to receive a name by others; this is part of the process of being fully born. The United States of America did not exist before they were called the United States of America. This remains ununderstandable to a Greek mind. And the Cartesian blindness to this reality of names disfigures most investigations of psychologists, sociologists and historians who do not know that they are paralyzed by their Cartesian origins.

So far we have introduced three conjunctions into our analysis: *ergo, quia, ut*. These conjunctions in themselves offer nothing spectacular. "Therefore," "because" and "so that" do not transcend the prose of everyday logic. It is different with the term *etsi*, "although." No pagan logic admits the "although." The Christian era has added this step into novelty and continued creation. Newness is not man-made. Manufacturing combines known things by "because," "therefore," and "so that." But that we may become changed men, *although* we suffer, *although* we have to suffer, aye, even to die, is incomprehensible to a Greek mind and yet it is the everyday experience of any living soul.

In the *respondeo*, although I may be changed, the scientific mentality is transcended. Already the scholastics, especially Bonaventura, saw clearly the insufficiency of the Greek mind. The Greeks tried to judge us from things; hence, their apes could coin the ridiculous phrase of a *res cogitans*. Creativity comes to self-forgetfulness. He who remains inside his own consciousness is impotent, incapable of experiencing real newness. The old consciousness must die, must be abandoned, must be forgotten in the passionate surrender to an unforeseen situation. Necessity overcomes the impossible. That which hitherto has been deemed impossible demonstrates the prison walls of today's consciousness. It is by the strange conjunction of "although" that the new necessity overwhelms the most reactionary part of our organism, *id est*, our obstinate "consciousness."

"Our little systems have their day." Our own regeneration, the regeneration of knowledge, and the progress of science are conditioned by the application of the non-Greek conjunction, "although." Although nobody has thought this possible hitherto, it is true just the same, is the most general formula for the continuous renewal of human thinking. In this grammatical form, consciousness takes second seat and stands corrected by the martyr, the discoverer, the naive, and the good Samaritan. All these types act "although" that which they do has never been done before and therefore is classified as impossible.

Most of modern methodology skips this test of originality, the courage to say "although." To the Christian Era, only this mind may be said to belong, who has the guts to defy his own consciousness by the nobility of his passion, by the energy of his research, by the selfless courage of the Billy Mitchells.[3] The chain of events which we call the history of science is formed by these steps which, in complete self-forgetfulness, lead man beyond his self-consciousness.

[3] A famous flyer of World War I who accepted being courtmartialed for his bold criticism of the Air Force.

Of "disinterestedness," much has been said in the 19th century. The term will not do in an era of monetary corruption. "I respond although this will demand my own transformation," my own loss of position, is the only methodological protection against the cheap research of the modern masses of academic proletarians. They must be left behind; their naive interest in themselves is not good enough.

Our old Adam, our inherited mentality, has to be shed and left behind by the *etsi*, the "although." Bonaventura has called this "an excess of the mind," a getting beside ourselves. It is the condition of any progress. *The quadrilateral of man as thinking, as being an extended substance, as being a listener, only is completed when we make room inside ourselves for being made over.* The term "creative" nowadays is the fashion. It is meaningless, as we certainly are not God almighty, but very mortal, very corrupt and terribly stupid. The term "creative" will lead the people astray, unless they recognize that we only may become creative by transcending the boundaries of our own yesterday-logic, by responding to a need although it demands our own abandon.

The reader has found at the beginning of this essay the quadrilateral of a revised logic. The two times, from the beginning to me, and from the end to me, are represented by the *audio ut fiam* (listening completes my historical existence) and the *respondeo etsi mutabor.*

As "subject" and "object" are conceived in the Greek versions *cogito ergo sum, mensuror quia existo,* so we may label the heroes of the second pair of statements "traject" and "preject." The Quadrilateral, the Cross of Reality, to sum it all up, demands and requires that we remain willing to be alternatingly "object," "subject," "traject," "preject." And we may add that there are four religions possible, according to the priority given to any of these four attitudes of man.

CHAPTER 6

THE TWELVE TONES
OF THE SPIRIT[1]

SPIRIT AND LOVE ARE STRONGER than death. Hence, we cannot do without them unless we condemn ourselves to sterile futility. For to love means to become fruitful, and to be inspired means to overcome and to limit death. When the body dies, the spirit remains. The spirit proves itself to be divine whenever the trails blazed by creative, loveable lives are travelled by deliberate successors, heirs, pupils, followers, or when devilish trails are renounced and abandoned by warning posts: No trespassing!

Hence, the ultimate test of the spirit is the heritage of newly acquired faculties which future generations gratefully receive and accept. All the various expressions of our faith: presence of God, future, regeneration, adoption, children of God, not of Man, the very terms liberty, God, Spirit, Devil, history—have tried to transmit to us this good news that we had predecessors who have endowed us with acquired faculties, acquired by them and bestowed on us if we only respond by accepting them. Also, the good news was contrasted with the bad news. And without the bad news, the good news is ununderstandable. Perhaps the good news will more readily become audible again after we speak explicitly about the bad news. The bad news says that a child is better than a hoary head, that new is better than old, that stimulation and sensation drag us along from day to day as they presume to guarantee us better values. This bad-

[1] An address to members of St. Augustine Church, Santa Monica, California, 1961.

ness is very bad indeed. The truth is that neither is the child better than the old man nor is the old man better than the child. God is incalculable. He makes some children and some adults very good indeed and others, elders or children, very wicked. He is incalculable and certainly is quite indifferent to the date or year at which we are born. It is equally difficult at all times to live the good life.

The good news, in emphasizing this complete indifference of God to the year of our birth or our death, also says that we, in following the trail blazed by the Firstborn Son, may become the people of His inheritance. Hence the good news is related to a perpetual relation of founder and heir, of testator and successors. This truth is obscured today. Even the old term "Imitation of Christ" has been weakened. Too often it is understood not as the inheritance of Christ's acquired faculty but as a pedantic imitation and aping. Let us restate the good news.

Christ has acquired a new faculty, the timing of the Spirit. And he has imparted to us this rightly timed spirit, this power not only to talk, to think, to write, to proclaim, to sing, but also to obey these promptings in God's good time, neither too early nor too late.

Here, I forego the temptation to accuse the naturalists of robbery and plagiarism. I could accuse them of having embezzled all our terms of the Spirit's life, presence, future, heredity, survival, history, acquired faculties. Originally, all these terms of Darwin hail from the Bible. Because only God can be present. Only the children of his inheritance can have a future, only the fruits of the spirit can survive death. And only the apostles can succeed in transmitting the newly acquired faculties of our Savior. But I shall leave it to you to draw these conclusions yourselves.

However, I may perhaps have to remind you that in society, in our historical community, we move as men born through the living Word into our times and places, into our future destiny. We have the singular privilege of contributing to the everlasting survival of acquired faculties which we embrace and to contribute to the everlasting relegation to hell of those acquired faculties which we wish to see extirpated. Thus, Creation is taking place under our very noses. And nobody can stay neutral in this spiritual war between bequeathing the good qualities to the future through faith or giving up from despair the task of weeding out the diabolical qualities.

The way by which we are threaded into God's creation, day after day, that is into his history, is through the twelve stages or tones of the Spirit. Because God's processes are known to everybody, nobody seems to pay much attention to their beautiful order and ineluctable sequence. No generation seems to have been so callous about this process as ours. Impatiently and with great haste, the whole inspiration is sold to us over the counter. "Inspiration" is advertised, pointed out to us as Inspiration Point, etc. But, alas, inspiration takes time. It must fill ninety or a hundred years of a long life. Is it not highly probable that the Spirit befalls us, through a long life, in very many variations? You know as well as I that the Spirit permeates our carnal bodies in at least three steps: He enters into us. This stage is called childhood. Everything, in this phase, is received by the child with the zest of "first-ness"; "new" equals "inspiration," during childhood.

Then, however, this spirit begins to work in us. He stirs us up. He abides in us and transforms us. This phase we may call adulthood. Lastly, the Spirit being a power cannot be secluded inside of us. He holds forth, he proceeds outside. This stage we may call elderhood, or with the Greek corresponding term, priesthood.

Upward was the Spirit in every child of Adam. Inward he operates in every man or woman when they come of age. Outward from us upon society when we hold office. Today, this tripartition does not suffice. We must be more specific. The numerous processes of the Spirit have not been discerned very clearly since the Reformation. Perhaps, the second article of the Creed, i.e. the sentences on the Savior, have monopolized the labors of theologians. The philosophers, on the other hand, have usurped the first article and by isolating it, they have made it meaningless. But the third article of the Creed is the first article of our experience. The apostles experienced the Father through the Son in the Holy Spirit. In other words, before God came upon them as the spirit of Pentecost, neither the Son nor the Father was accessible to them. The strange yearnings of the Pentecostal sects of our times should warn us that an experience of the spirit will have to precede any understanding of either Son or Father in the Trinity. The legitimate Church must fight the Greek arrogance by which our so-called minds are not considered the receptacle, the vehicle, or the carrier of the One Spirit through the ages, but as the free agents of our little atomized, innumerable, different selves.

When we approach the mental processes in ourselves as the process of the Spirit from others usward, within us and from usward to others, an order of three times four spiritual attitudes will become audible. The dying man, when he gives back the spirit to his Creator, is allowed by our laws to leave behind a last will and testament. This is the minimum spiritual honor the community vouchsafes him. Hence, the spiritual life of all of us should be traced from our dying hour backward. While in "nature" birth seems to precede death, and life is described as the sum of all the processes this side of dying, the Spirit reverses this order of naturalism.

> In nature, birth precedes death;
> In nature, life tries to shun death.
> In the spirit, death precedes life;
> In the spirit, the founder's death guides his heirs' lives.

Hence, the first spiritual command is: leave a will, endow, bequeath. This is the first command because it gives direction and meaning to all our previous steps. He who experiences his dying day as fulfillment is blessed. Therefore, this person, whatever he believes to be bliss, he will project backwards from his dying day upon his antecedents. He will wish to have this fulfillment from the whole time span of life. Once we unlock this secret door of the spiritual order in Christianity, we suddenly understand why Christ indeed unlocked the gates of death to our soul.

Our dying day and our supreme will and legacy are directed towards future generations; from this fact we may easily illuminate all the previous stages of life. The last commandments must dominate all earlier ones. After all, they shall enable us to make our perfect will, that ultimate will by which the human inheritance may be increased and by which it may become the fruit of our lives' seed.

The stage of testator therefore will usually be preceded by

> prophet or warner
> teacher or educator
> leader or legislator
> sufferer or perseverer
> protester or rebel
> critic or analyst
> doubter or despondent
> player or singer
> learner or wanderer
> reader or conceiver
> listener or obeyer

This order has been forgotten in secularism. In application by the secular thinker, the spiritual order is reversed. In secular psychology which begins with the child itself, we are told that it should pull itself up by its own bootstraps and become itself, express itself, live by itself. Of this the inexorable consequence must be that it will have to live and may also have to die by, for and unto itself. A horrid spectacle indeed.

When the learning of speech is seen as the twelfth spiritual tone, i.e. as the first intimate of the Spirit when He enters a newborn soul, then we perceive that this tone wells up, in man's life, so to speak from his death bed. The child's first smile is on the other end at the farthest distance from Jesus' words on the Cross or from the farewell address of George Washington, or from the last speech of Moses. The tone of the spirit reverberates first within us when we obey. The child which is not made to obey is denied the power ever to command. To command, to identify ourselves with God's will, is our perfection, our destination. Any person who makes a will, in any field of human endeavor, commands, or, better still, becomes a command. Lincoln, Cardinal Newman, Moses are commanding figures after death. All their powers seem to have gone into that part of them which during their lives they could not realize. The greatness of Moses lies in just this, that he did not enter the promised land himself. In this lies the divinity of Christ, that he did not use the Spirit for his own time but gave this spirit to the apostolic succession.

Having thus restored the twelfth command, "listen" or "obey" to its rank as the corollary to the first command, "leave your spirit to posterity," we shall have no trouble in dividing the keyboard between the twelfth command and the first into approximately ten periods of about six years each and three periods of about twenty years each.

I.   Youth or childhood; in society represented by the artist.
12. obey   existential   involved
11. read   mental   detached
10. learn   selective   half involved, half detached
 9. sing   all this time, as your hour has not yet come

II. Adulthood; in society represented by the fighter.
 8. doubt and withhold   half involved, half detached
 7. analyze and synthesize detached
 6. speak up and insist   get involved
 5. wait and persevere   stay engaged

III. The Elders; the universal priesthood of the believers.
 4. lead and legislate
 3. teach and instruct
 2. prophesy and warn
 1. "testate" endow and bestow

All twelve commandments or tones of the Spirit permeate all the phases of our life. A camp counsellor obviously may be 19 and yet act in the capacity of tone 4 or 3 already. This does not alter the fact that each tone should be given one period of life for its fullest cultivation. When children of 12 are trained for leadership, it only goes to show that the educators, psychologists, politicians heap all the crowns of adult and elder on youngsters who must perish under this burden.

Of each time, a whole book could and might be written. For instance, "teach" is a "must" in any maturing person's life.

Man must teach. Once this is understood, the raising of
teachers will appear to be infinitely more difficult than the
raising of children or the building of school palaces. Also it will
become clear that we teach what our students are meant to do,
to carry out, to uphold, to render because we cannot do it all
ourselves. In other words, there is a proportion between governors and teachers. The father is the governor, the teacher, and
the prophet as well as the testator for the next generation. He
leads them into the future, teaches about the future, prophesies
the calamities or obstacles on their way into the future, and
tries to leave them some means for coping with this future. All
this belongs to his priestly office.

Hence commands 1, 2, 3, 4 (testate, prophesy, teach, rule)
are one and the same command spelled out in its four aspects!
The same is true of the 4 commands for the fighting adults and
the four commands of childhood.

Also, at close harkening, the reader may observe that children,
adults, elders or artists, fighters, priests—are in a different phase
with regard to timing. A child plays and is not yet serious because it "has time," more precisely because its day has not yet
come. The meaning of play is that the play remains this side
of the process by which God proceeds in wars, calamities, crises,
revolutions.

Children have infinite, more precisely, "undefined" time.
Conversely, the fighters press on. They try to be ahead of their
times. They are impatient. As a Protestant should try to hurry
the coming of the Day of the Lord. Paul wants us to be impatient as well as patient, because we are both children who
play before God and fighters who fight for God. The relation
of the elder to time again is different. His genius is in the
timing. Between the abolitionists (the "adults") and the indifferent ones (the playboys) Lincoln proved to be the good
governor because of his timing. He timed the emancipation of
the slaves to perfection, to the perfection prophesied thirty
years before by John Quincy Adams. Adams prophesied that
the slavery issue after 1828 had reached an impasse which only
the commander-in-chief in a time of war could break. This, by
the way, is a good illustration of the genuine role of prophecy

in the spiritual process. Prophecy is not prediction or forecasting the weather. Prophecy speaks from the last Judgment Day backwards into our own days. Hence, it always places between our today and our last day some terrible calamity. For the prophet acknowledges that the present generation does not move in the direction of our destiny. Judging the present in the light of our destiny, he knows that the obstacles thrown up by our moving in the wrong direction first must be removed. Prophets then are not predicting how to get rich but prophesying that our heirs will be visited for our own greed or trespassing.

The prophet, then, is as intimately connected with the future as governors, teachers, or testators. Moses, Isaiah, Ecclesiastes, King Jonas, Stephen, John, Luke, Peter, the first four in the Old, the second four in the New Testament are united although we may discern among them kings, teachers, prophets, and testators. Because all of them live out of the future, out of the solidarity of God's creature Man, into their present day.

When we would recognize them as the tones one, two, three, four on the Spirit's harp, the childishness of our educational situation today might easily be conquered. For then it will be seen that a child cannot learn to speak by swallowing nouns, mere words, but only by carrying out orders existentially. The verbs are the root words by which the child is put in action. Our machine age with push button mechanizing is threatening our children because, instead of enacting the verbs go, push, pull, tear, lift, answer, speak, write, move, climb, etc., the child is surrounded by dead things which by one and the same motion can be made to respond.

We cannot become eloquent unless we enact the words spoken to us existentially.

CHAPTER 7

HERACLITUS TO PARMENIDES

Preface

THE FOLLOWING LETTER IS NEITHER fiction nor forgery. It is a conjuration. A deep mental sickness of our time is attacked and conjurement or exorcism is not an unheard-of cure. In a strange obduration of our vision, we are taking it for granted that anybody born in Greece between Homer and Plotinus had to have a "Greek" mentality, unalloyed by Jewish, id est prophetic and monotheistic elements. On the other hand, we are not surprised to find that in Israel, the Egyptian or the Canaanitic or Greek features have often eclipsed the genuine Israelitic function.

The approach to the peculiarly Greek errancy (as the Greek Fathers of the Church called the Odyssey of the Greek mind in retrospect), which we here propose, is a different one. From Homer to Parmenides the road was still open, the door to a common spirit of man was not closed. Solely after or with Parmenides did the metaphysical prison start in which subject and object, mind and body, nature and society were forever split. From Parmenides to Heidegger a time-continuum exists and whoever enters this maze called metaphysics or even philosophy, loses his membership in the pre-Greek humanity. In revenge, he calls this pre-Greek humanity primitive or uncivilized or barbaric. It is true that all philosophical terms are of Greek origin as the term philosophy itself is; logic, ethics, physics, theology, all are Greek terms and products of the mind that beginning with Parmenides seceded from the rest of the race as peculiarly Greek and is found in all "sophisticated" minds today.

The point of embarkation—and this is no accident but occurs at any such decisive epoch—was marked off by Heraclitus. Heraclitus was left behind by the philosophy of "being" and by the record of his protest we have the means of finding our own bearings when overwhelmed by the lures of "reason" in our own age or in any age. The Christian Fathers have given Heraclitus this honor of having been a Christian before Christianity. And when the socialists—after Hegel—tried to free mankind from the fetters of abstraction and ideology—Ferdinand Lassalle chose Heraclitus as his "Great Argument" in contrast to Marx who attacked the modern Parmenides of his day, Hegel. Every time has its new form of sophistry and philosopher. We have symbolic logic, we have Heidegger and Sartre. And again, Heraclitus may save us. Aye, it seems to me that this time, once for all, we may really break the vicious circle of the metaphysicians. Thanks to the sufferings of the last forty years, the bluff of metaphysics can be called. There is one more hurdle in our way. They whose jargon nobody can control or check, have nicknamed the simple and political and straightforward Heraclitus "The Dark" lest anybody read him. For the naive, primitive, normal member of any community, Heraclitus is simple, and the gentlemen from Parmenides to Heidegger are the ones who sit in the smoke-filled room of their own definitions. Hence the following document is composed with the utmost respect for our sources and tries to conjure up the eternal issue in terms which identify our situation and the situation in 500 B.C.

Heraclitus of Ephesus to Parmenides of Elea

Ephesus, On the day of Zeus thunders

My Parmenides,

You kindly wrote to me of your new generalizations. One of them you call "the being," to which you oppose that which should not be, *mee on*. And you request my opinion.

If I was the gruff man they pretend me to be, I would simply say the new term "the being" is the only *mee on* to me, the one term which we should never use, because it was not meant to be said or thought by mortal man. But I am not as gruff and I see you and me quite well defined, standing in a totally different situation and therefore aiming at the very opposite types of articulating.

My point of view and your point of view are *loci standi*, and we do not stand in the same place. I once found myself as the legitimate appointed first mayor of our free port and city. I have succeeded into a succession of illustrious names and offices of the past. Your words aim at the minds of young men who still play around. They do not yet serve their country under any specific appointment or name. You, so to speak, address that element in a man with which he still is a student before graduation. To the man before he is initiated you address your generalizations.

My aim has been to speak to those who can think because they have been appointed. In practice, this may seem to be quibbling. Your reader may be as old as mine. But to talk to a man on the first day after he has taken office and to generalize for him as I have tried to do, so that he may find his way in the maze of innumerable contradictory functions, is one thing. And to speak to men to whom the whole universe is still on undivided space because the powers that be protect them in their wanderings and musings, as you speak, is quite another. Their universe is a world of play.

Let me prove this first of all. You meet minds at play. For the real world is not one undivided space. The knowledge of the real world is entrusted to men after they have cut out paths through times and spaces by their bestowing names, rank, and degree to those with whom they live, in mutual recognition. All knowledge of the world is predicated on mutual recognition by name and introduction to each other. Of my listeners I have thought as people who had experienced how names opened up opportunity, how they stipulated in so many words as were required to perform so many acts among themselves. They would address each other by name so as to let each other pass or block the way. They would give orders, the orders of their office, so that it may be done and then enacted as having been done at such and such a date. My listeners, then, use names to help or to obstruct each other, and they use verbs to begin or to end an act within society. They respect verbs not as statements of facts but because they make us turn agenda into acts, acts into facts, and conjugation is the purpose of their speech.

It is the illusion of the open heath, of the empty walls of study halls, to think of words as devoid of action, of action as possible outside of speech. This illusion now is nourished by you, Parmenides. Your term "being" tries to make the playgrounds sovereign. Let me explain to you how I feel about the waterfall of unpolitical thought which you are about to unleash. You will perhaps admit then that I am not ignorant of the relative truth of your procedure but that it strikes me as absurd that you try to give it the primacy in truth. Therefore, I first have to give the devil his due. Yes, you may talk about anything under the sun in your theories, Parmenides. But you cannot alter the fact that there always remains a difference of the first order between speech and talk. This distinction consists in *the form* of these two manners of expression. Speech is formal, talk is informal. Some truth cannot be expressed informally. But you proceed to do it just the same. Hence, a foreshortening of the truth must result if the formal, "highbrow" truths of courthouse and temple, council and army are translated into the informal language of academic discussion and private dialogue and fireside chats.

In our nurseries and playgrounds, after meals and in the bosom of the family, we do not speak but talk. The speaker is in harness in the uniform of his office; the talker is in shirtsleeves and slippers. For to talk means to have relaxed. While we relax, we may be informal. The same judge who sends a murderer to the gallows, may crack informally a joke five minutes later. But he cannot pass the sentence by talk nor may he joke by using formal language. And here you see the dilemma. The judge *cannot* pass his sentence validly except by using formal language. But he could blaspheme against the sanctity of his office by playing with its formulas. Only he "may" not if he wishes to be a good judge. Everything hinges on this distinction between "can" and "may." Formal speech *may* not be used by the magistrates as a joke. Informal talk *cannot* be used by the officers when officiating. You cannot pass sentence by talking off the record. You may not pass the time by undermining the sanctity of your office.

Our children play hopscotch. This is a play which imitates the serious procession of the dead through heaven and hell, when they are brought before their judges in the after-life as we were taught by the Egyptian priests. The distinction between speech and talk would never be lost if we still lived in the days of the ancients when neither women nor children spoke at all. But now everybody learns language. And now, the forms of the law and of worship are extensively played with by the young. In fact, all our children toy with the legal processes of their elders. They play marriage and war and pawnshop, and due process of law, in their playing with the forms and categories there established. And in their childish tongue, the distinction between the forms which may not be used and which cannot be used, vanishes. Therefore, let me make this distinction between formal speech and informal talk the main topic of my letter. For if children could fuse low-brow and high-brow *ad libitum,* your choice of the term "being" would be impeccable. It would just round out the vocabulary of informal thinking. To me, however, the realm of informal talk cannot transgress certain limitations. That it is impossible to say the things of greatest importance arbitrarily and informally, may be seen from a list of examples.

When I sent an embassy to Miletus, my messengers probably said rather informally, as we are good friends: "We have come to tell you such and such." But the stark truth behind their informal talk was the herald's or the usher's formal calling out: "The ambassadors from Ephesus," and the formal address of their credentials: "To the People of Miletus," lest they be liars. When a child says "daddy" and "mommy," the stark truth behind these informal words is that the parents are the child's father and child's mother and that a public record actually calls them so. The public record cannot speak of daddy and mommy; for the opening of a common life is granted to those only who are called fathers and mothers in our city.

You have written to me about your find because I am Heraclitus and you are Parmenides. There is more persistence in your being Parmenides than in the "you" applied to Parmenides by Heraclitus in this present letter. Somewhere this, your official name, must occur although I may not use it in the context of the letter at all. For simplicity's sake, we here speak of you and I and me, and wallow in informality. Similarly, at our symposia, we may rant and curse that something is rotten, and the wicked will be acquitted anyway. Nevertheless, in back of such "somethings" and "anyways," definite misdemeanors must be understood. When I get up in the market place, I cannot simply say that something is wrong. I must say whether the mayor is a tyrant, or the *demos* anarchical, or the judges corrupt.

Informal speech can never identify reality to its highest possible degree. Neither "I," nor "you," nor "he" nor "it" are the complete procedure for identification. They are pronouns. The list,

daddy	mommy
I	you
he	it
this	that
anyway	somehow
Jennie	Mike

is a list of pro-nouns which we use instead of nouns when we talk informally.

Pronouns are a compromise between the real name of a person or a thing and the pointing finger while such person or thing is within the reach of our sense perception. To call a spade a spade is one thing; to point to the spade while it lies before us, which simply requires the gesture and a "there!," is a totally different act. One is the act of naming, the other is an attempt to reduce naming to its informal minimum.

Keep these two situations in mind: the solemn way of call-

ing out names while in our temples or at our gatherings, and
the animal ways of crying and whistling, and you will no
longer overestimate the compromise affected between the two
by the young. In the presence of folks or food, the animal
cub and his mother get by with grunting and barking and
whistling. Our children compromise and we the parents gladly
compromise with them, whenever we use pronouns, nicknames,
slang, between the full names of the initiated and the laziness
of the private home.

Forgive me when I repeat once more, in contrast, that nobody can function in his office unless his name is recognized.
I must repeat this because from there we may go on to your
generalization's strange assault on life's functioning.

The mariner calls out: gangway for the doctor, and that
may save a sick sailor's life. The political power of names
makes people circulate. Names signify our division of labor.
They make room for a man and a thing. The "throne," the
"hustings," our "tongue" as Greeks, the "eye of justice," the
"thunder of Zeus," those were all names whose invocation
made people move out or in. I understand that, among you,
the words for "things" are thought of as mere etiquettes for
physical objects. And "mother tongue," "the eye of God,"
"the thunder of Zeus," you call metaphors. For heaven's sake,
Parmenides, "mother tongue" is the original meaning of
tongue. A chair or throne was a throne first before it ever
was a "thing." *Speech* is creative metaphor. And only *talk* is
emptying thrones, tongues, hands, thunders, into mere physical objects. But let me be forgiven for getting angry at this
point. For it was not my purpose to digress about the priority
of metaphor. What I really wish to agree with you on is the
necessity that all names are reciprocal.

Names make no sense unless they stand in mutual relation.
Mother is not mother unless she may call, under the law,
somebody the father. Brother is brother to a sister. And unless
he calls her sister and she calls him brother, the name is
worthless. The general and the sergeant, the master and the
apprentice, the army and the navy make room for each other,
in the wonderful whole of names. All names belong to this

holon, to society. No name is good without the others. The
Pan of the universe drives people panicky, that is they lose
speech. The *holon* of the city gives everybody a name in such
a manner that everybody else now can be named by him, too.

When men philosophize about the world, the whole nomenclature of real titles, offices and names must be on their minds
before they may generalize. Zeus and Artemis are the Gods
of Ephesus. Only informally, we talk of them as "the divine."
The divine comes in handy when we dislike to be solemn. But
it has to be added to the list of pronouns. Neuters are one
more version of the eternal pronoun of our informal nature.
Why? Because Zeus and Artemis are reciprocal interests, "the
divine" has lost its mutuality of functioning names. Nobody
can be sure to what other part of reality "the divine" recipro-
cates. To those who never have invoked one single God, fearful to use the right name for him, *the* divine does not mean
a thing.

Please allow me to sum up the argument as it has unfolded
so far. There are three stages of linguistics: animal sounds,
formal speech, informal talk. The step which separates the
animal world from man is not the step from the rooster's cry
to the baby's lullaby. It is in the jump from a sound to a
name. In the formal world of names, all names are reciprocal
and make room for speakers and answers or give way to each
other, in one holon. Then rises the realm of the informal, in
which words lie together as the toys of a child in the circle
on the beach, encyclopedically, and that is without reciprocity
of speakers and listeners.

There could be no informal speech unless we had created
and did retain formal speech. Names have priority over pronouns. One cannot derive names from pronouns. Names are
free creations; pronouns are natural derivatives.

By now, I hope that I have convinced you that the low-
brow is the reflection of the highbrow, in the mind of the
young, the relaxed, the players. Unless I have convinced you,
the second half of this letter on "being" itself will not satisfy
you. For in this second half I intend to apply the findings

for our names to the meaning of verbs, in human speech. The noun-pronoun relation is of old standing. But you now parallel this relation by a verb-proverb relation. And this is new.

We have gotten over the shock of daddy and mommy and "it rains" for Zeus rains. But that Zeus who thunders, shall be said to "have being," Artemis who hunts, to be subsumed under "being," shocks us still. You say that verbs may be turned into an omnibus ersatz pro-verb, as names may become pronouns. As the children play with the city, so you invite us to play with the gods.

What of it, you will reply. Is this not ineluctable? It is the obvious trend of evolution.

My Parmenides, Gods are not men. Two facts about the Gods make them different from mortal men. And "being" will forever dampen the crowd's eagerness to learn of these two facts. What are they? The first is: we meet the Gods in the opposite manner from our fellow-men. The other is equally important: no one God is always with us.

As to point one, may it suffice to say this. When a man approaches us from afar and we cannot recognize him, he already is a man to us though not yet identified. Then he begins to act and then we specify who he is. With Gods, it is the other way. Their acts are the only facts known of the Gods. We see them in their acts first and never see much more of them. Tremendous movements of army against army allow us to say that Ares rages. The harvest's bounty shows us how Demeter blessed our fields. As a result of this difference between Gods and men, we are satisfied to give names to people. *Names never suffice for Gods*. It is their specific act which compels us to believe in the specific God. And it is the actuality created by the God's activity which compels us to worship the reciprocal Goddess. Surrounded by majestic catastrophes and bounties, we speak of the Gods in as far as acts stage our human drama, and we speak of Goddesses as we are made secure by the actualities created around such dramatic action. The cities and the virtues and the processes of law are the recurrent actualities of our Gods' initial acts.

Take away these acts of the Gods and the actualities of our *akropoleis*, our temples, our laws, and the wide earth becomes ineffable again.

The Gods have acted all the verbs which now form the matrices of our vocabulary. For verbs preserve the acts of Gods, not men. The verb and the specific verb is the lifeblood of a God. He commands, he blesses and he rises and he curses and he thunders. He exalts and he humiliates. Always does he become known in his act and never outside of it. Our point of contact with the Gods is in their acts. This has a grave consequence. Humans can drop their official masks. They can play. The Gods as far as they come into our lives never play with their function. We have no other way of coping with their acts except by taking them seriously. Homer has the Gods relax, I know, but this is not his source of information for the Gods. Of men we know after we have met them at games, and in the privacy of the home. Here, the playground is the best introduction; not so with Gods. If you ever wish to meet him, forget the manner of being introduced to your friends. The Gods cannot be known outside their serious acts.

Your term, "being," however, plays with all verbs. This, no God can survive. You take his scalp when you suppress his act.

Point two is even more readily overlooked. As the God acts, his act comes *kairoi*. At the appointed instant, his act makes its entrance and its exit. Today, he thunders, tomorrow he lifts Ganymedes to Olympos. Yesterday, Poseidon raged against Odysseus. Tomorrow, Hermes will go to Kalypso and consult with her on the hero's homecoming. We pray or deprecate the future acts of the Gods, we prophesy their approach, we thank them for their fulfillment in our festivals. This means that any God acts at his appointed hour. They befall us and they leave us again. And we are challenged to use a certain acuteness of our time sense. Now, that the Gods act is enshrined in our verbs. And this is obvious. It is less obvious that the appointed hour also is embalmed in the matrices of all our spirit. Is it not the wonderful form of any verb that it cannot help expressing the appointed hour by placing us either before, or in, or after the event? In this sense, I have spoken of Fire. It was, I wrote, and it is, and it shall be. For Gods pass and return.

Alas, my own step of lumping all the acts of the Gods together when I said: it was, it is, it shall be, now may be held against me. "Why do you bear a grudge against Parmenides? Is not your word, it was, it is, it shall be, as weak a term as any pronoun? Is it not exactly the omnibus pro-verb, this 'instead-of-all-specific-verbs' which you fear in Parmenides?"

Well do I know that I may be accused of heralding your own innovation. But while your "being" may make people think of Gods outside their acts, I felt that none of my citizens could slip in this manner as long as the act kept its refreshing unexpectedness before, and now, and after. Thus, you never are sure. "Fire" is uncertain in its central character. It is extinguishable, although it flares up again. And I was in deadly earnest with my generalizations. On the crossroads of the earth, our city has introduced so many exotic crafts and guilds that *the reciprocity of all* their professions had to be freshly stressed. The ebb and tide of everybody's participation in the life of the *holon,* I tried to drive home.

Your term "being," however, is not the result of such a pressure for political harmony. It is a mirror of life, no medicine for its confusions. With the Gods, their appointed hour is our appointment with our destiny. "Being" is indifferent to the God's appointment with us. His absence or his presence you suggest shall make no difference. "Being" is good enough for spectators of life. But men must know when Gods ask us to speak, and when to fall silent. To children on whose lips no God ever placed any words and never silenced them with awe, "being" is as good a word about reality as "he" for the king, and "she" for the maid. But "it" is not a word for any God as it wipes off our brow the sweat of fear and trembling and expectation and despair.

This, then, is the manner of real speech, that he who tries to join a living community of speaking members must humbly ask what is going on. Our words for the question what, who, how, where, etc., are all fillers and they are whispered with no less breath and emphasis than the known parts of the sentence. The man who asks for the road to Ephesus, must say: where does the road to Ephesus go? And he thereby shows that he cannot complete the sentence himself. He already knows the name of Ephesus or road and the word go. But "where" is to be thrown out by the competent answerer who, as a full-fledged resident of the place, can distinguish Miller's Pond from Hangman's Corner. The resident, in his answer, directs the outsider so that he is enabled to complete the sentence: the road to Ephesus leads by Hangman's Corner.

Real speech, then, gives the man second rank. To ask is to look for fuller information by those who know. This normal service of question and answer, that it is a feeder into participation in a going concern, is perverted in your students' manners. You now ask the ignorant and promise that the experts will be enriched by the answer of the ignorant. This sophistry makes the question an independent act which no longer presupposes somebody who can be asked because he knows. The revolution will shake every commonwealth. For the know-nothings now are not only asking the questions but they now feel unencumbered by any existing answer.

Parmenides, Parmenides, by making him who must ask, at the same time that man who also can give the answer, law and government will become impossible. The gymnasiums filled with naked, beautiful but inexperienced boys will proclaim their own untested truth as the answer is given there and not sought from those who do not have to ask because they have mastered the replies by their actions and habits since time immemorial.

You detach the students from the wise, the young from the old, and the ingenious tapestry of life between the many generations of man is replaced by a wild scramble of contemporary boys without memory and their flatterers, admirers and bought tutors among the old. For such a crowd of men who live by curiosity and who answer their own questions in an obscene self-love, the only way out is your way: to proclaim generalizations like "being," abstracts like "it" and "they."

I did generalize, too, but I still did it for the adult and

officiating citizens. Everyone of our guilds and crafts—to say nothing of judges, priests, captains, and police—every activity in our city has come into existence because a God sponsored their acts. Pray, said the God, and the priest prayed. Bake, tailor, hunt, guard, the God commanded, and he who baked became the baker, he who tailored became the tailor, he who hunted became the hunter of our good city. Without this obedience to Hephaistos, Hermes, Zeus, no *poietes* would work the statues of the Gods, no merchant would go to market, no judge would uphold the Themis. In the division of labor of our city, every citizen got his good conscience from the verbs. They explained to him the rhythm, the beginning and the end of his activities within the sacred calendar and liturgy of the whole. Our city moves in the trance of a cosmic dance in which judge and baker know their password because of their names.

I have tried to purify this dance and to prevent confusion, by assigning to every member his rise and fall, his going and returning. The city requires both, great zest and transient zest. The most eager judge must stop when meal time has come. Where many must act seriously, yet differently and at different times, I tried to restate the commonwealth's paradox of *transient zest*. The appointed hours and the appointed offices must both be brought on by us; for this reason our names and titles are specific and formal, and our acts are God-ordered and God-rescinded. The names of the Gods and the names of men are reciprocal. Neither means anything by itself.

You, Parmenides, have abandoned the serious liturgy of city life. You wish to *see* the Gods. For this contemplation which you take to the playground, you send the times on vacation. You are like the barker in front of the circus who promises a magic mirror of the universe. The man who enters his booth relaxes. He loses his identity. He is one of the crowd. The people is changed into the public.

The public is a bunch of cowards always. Your boys now can debate about the universe without the fear of blasphemy. It may be an interesting topic in the palestra whether the divine has "being." The council of our city must try to find out whether Zeus blesses or curses, whether Hera sends discord or peace.

You treat as a topic of relaxation the very acts which never relax. Out of the affairs of the community you produce generalizations. You complete the secession of our playboys from our citizens. For this reason, I have to draw the line between you and me.

I still try to speak to everybody as a citizen who at any time may officiate. You address the informal daddy or kid in all of us. For by now you will not deny that the *scalping of names*, in which you have taken the last step, is permissible solely to those who talk, never to those who speak. "Being" is the scalp of the divine acts and the political names. This scalp hangs dangling from your belt. To hell with your "pronoun," to hell with your pro-verb "being." Or we all shall find ourselves in hell.

Heraclitus

CHAPTER 8

TEACHING TOO LATE,
LEARNING TOO EARLY[1]

IT IS MY PRIVILEGE here to report on a year-long campaign for
taking some timely steps at Dartmouth. However, I cannot
suppress the remark, at the outset, that my theme, "Teaching
too late, learning too early," has caught me in my own net.
Five years ago, when I spoke here first, I could not make myself understood; it was too early. And today is May 22nd.
Only a fool taps the resources of thinking, his own and others', at the last hour of the academic year; it is untimely to
try to do a good job today. We are dog-tired ourselves, in
a groggy and paralyzed western world.

However, as a typical teacher, here I stand and speak too
late.

1. *Timing*

I intend to make three points:

1. That the time has come to build up a science of timing,
   and that its *Novum Organum* will be the timing of
   teaching and learning, because they are its basic phenom-
   ena. Therefore, the new science must begin by reforming
   the teachers.

[1] An address given at the end of a professional seminar which was
held with thirty members of the faculty at Dartmouth College during
the academic year 1939–40, at the request of the Administration of
Dartmouth College.

2. That society is doomed without the timing of teaching, and that society is being destroyed around us daily—for lack of it—by brain erosion.
3. That every human being, for his own salvation, must be trained in the timing of all his experiences throughout life. Especially must he learn to fear being "too early" and "too late" as the greatest of sins.

Of course this is a mere program, and must serve as a program for many years to come. I throw these words over the barrier of the present war, and over the many hurdles of daily routine in politics and academic work, into the distant years of Dartmouth College. And I do so to save a future for Dartmouth.

Let me illustrate this by an anecdote. The Komburg is one of the most beautiful remnants of Romanesque art on the border of Franconia and Suabia. The Peasants' War that destroyed many neighboring towns in 1525 did not touch it. When, in Germany, we founded our first Academy of Adult Education on the Komburg, we learned the reason. Forty years before the Reformation, the Chapter had reformed itself voluntarily on the lines the Reformation was to follow. So the Chapter completely escaped the ravages of the German Revolution.

They broke the monastic rules in time. We must break the academic prejudices in time—though we have no forty years ahead of us.

These academic prejudices may be summed up as "obsession with space"—especially with external space and its corresponding ideal of "objectivity"—to the utter neglect of time. Our classrooms with their impossible benches and our division into departments represents the result of centennial space supremacy. Our college methods are all methods developed for space. And this is really disastrous in the humanities and social studies because man is peculiarly a temporal being, ever but an exile and a pilgrim in the world of space. Academic thinking has harnessed time to the triumphant chariot of space as a poor fourth dimension, and we habitually speak of "time spans," "length of time," etc. Recent Sophists have gone so far as to call our Real time "the spacious present." Let us look beyond Sophistry. In religion and in poetry an hour is filled with width as well as length. The very word "hour," this remnant of the ecclesiastical "*horae,*" decidedly still has a ring beyond its length of sixty minutes. An hour passed alone in silence is such a victory of man over his fears that Pascal calls it the precipice for our virtue. Real time is as full as mere space is empty.

This college is one of the best in the land; yet it is, at this moment, without a future; it is intentionally and wholly given to space realization. Objectivity is its god. It would treat all realities as things external to the mind, things in which we as thinkers have no roots, and which may accordingly be touched, weighed, measured, and manipulated without reference to the common destiny in which we and they are jointly bound. This may do for physics. It will not do for human society.

Fortunately our academic obsessions have been countered in recent decades by an increasing concern with time on the part of leading thinkers, and I appeal to them as evidence for the timeliness of a science of timing. All great new thought in our age centers around time; all great literature is trying to solve its riddles. At this tragic hour, when France's soul is bleeding away, it is well to remember that the Frenchman Bergson saved the soul of the last generation by reclaiming our plenitude of time. He has refuted the constant abuse of time by the space sciences; he has made it absurd to treat time as one-dimensional any longer—as the henchmen of space-science in the humanities and social studies still do.

But Bergson and Proust are not enough, in the light of the present catastrophe. They have not challenged our negligent habits of timing. It remained for a few younger thinkers, taking their cue from language, to restore due reverence for the fullness of time in all its glorious three tenses; not only the future and past, but also their common product, the present.[2] This supplies the fundamental method of the science of timing, and I shall apply it tonight.

The present, whether it be an hour, a day in our life, or a whole era, is not only created, but created by us; it does not simply happen to us, it is not a natural fact like space, not a datum in nature, but a constant social achievement, and neither comes nor lasts except by our own making. Therefore time is not a gift but a task; true presence of mind, the power to live in the fullness of time, is something that has to be won arduously and preserved by perpetual vigilance. Otherwise, our present is so starved and distorted that we can hardly be said to have one at all. Hence the cardinal importance of the problem of timing.

When man rises above his future, which is the imminence of his death, and beyond his past, which is the reminiscence of his origins, he enters the present. From the conflict of end and origin, of death and birth, the present results for those who have the courage not to blink but face the abyss before and in back of them. These courageous souls—the god-fearing, death-conquering few—are the creators of any present. We, the death-fearing, god-killing many, live on their courage and creativity; we follow them because the present emerging from their faith is dam and dyke against mere past and mere future, mere decay and mere revolution. Then we are more than our origin and our destination; we are.

And we *are* chiefly through the medium of human speech and conversation. Without participation in the life of the Word through the ages, we remain ephemeral. Speaking, thinking, learning, teaching, writing are the processes into which we must be immersed to become human "beings." They enable us to occupy a present in the midst of flux. Language receives us into its community; Speech admits us to the common boat of humanity, and we are clothed with permanence. By speaking we become the oarsmen of humanity in its strug-

[2] Franz Ebner, *Das Wort und die Geistigen Realitäten*, 1919; the present writer, *Angewandte Seelenkunde*, 1923, *Out of Revolution, Autobiography of Western Man*, 1938. A kindred development is the discovery of "biological time" by recent biologists: Lecomte de Nouy, *Biological Time*, 1939, London.

gle for orientation on its pilgrimage through space and time.

As speakers we are, under the condition that we are not just ourselves. I know too well that our churches have betrayed this source truth. But I wish to show you that we teachers must take up the truth that the ministers have abandoned, because otherwise we shall lose our right to teach. As true teachers we are not ourselves; rather the ages from Adam on speak through us into the future; and our listener too is not just himself in listening, but a link in the chain of speaking humanity until the last day of the created world. I do not speak here "for what my opinion is worth," as the belittling phrase goes, but because I make an honest attempt to let more than mere opinion reach you through me. Paradoxically, people who pretend that language is their own invention, that words are mere tools, are apt to lack personal force; the ones who make themselves into waves in the ocean of human speech through the ages acquire personal power as a by-product of their faith in the unanimity of mankind.

Man's dignity lies not in producing private opinions but in *timing* public truth. His speech must not only be more than himself: it must come at the right moment, in the fullness of time. Then his words acquire a "once for ever" meaning. All the sayings of Jesus were quite simple; they became important forever because they were spoken at the right moment, "when the time was fulfilled." A truth taught without the time element is abstract, therefore not vital. Truth is concrete at the lucky opportunity and hour. When we speak too late or too early we are out of luck; our truth remains abstract, and we fail to create a present in which people transcend mere past and future; we lack presence of mind. For these reasons teaching involves all the central problems of timing.

2. The Sins of Teaching and Learning

Our students "prepare" for life; we "postpare" it. The business of teaching is to be representative of all stages of the life of the human spirit except, of course, the one now present in the student. Teaching is therefore inevitably abstract, and hence in a sense always too late, as learning is too early. We teachers are the cultural lag of mankind. Less politely, we are the hyenas of its battlefields, for we disembowel the heroes of antiquity if we are left to our natural tendencies as teachers.

Let me stress this phrase, "left to our natural tendencies." We shall soon see why nobody on earth can be left to his natural tendencies. And you all know well that a good teacher is one who overcomes his natural inertia. But before studying the counterpoint used by all real teachers, we must first make the point that exploiting the things gone by and merely repeating them is our real temptation.

The devil capitalizes on this inertia, this natural gravity of teaching. One obvious example is our teaching about the World War. How many college men of the Western Powers have disemboweled the First World War till they were caught by the Second? They have thus annihilated the power of their students to live in the real present of the second.

In October 1939, the official scientific adviser to the British Conservative Party, Arthur Bryant, could publish a volume "Unfinished Victory," which dealt with the Treaty of Versailles in Hitler's arguments and from Hitler's "unfinished victory." The absence of mind in Great Britain was patently complete, so complete that instead of waging war my English academic friends came over to America to discuss with us the terms of the next peace. They were too late and too early at the same time as well.

Here in America we discovered in ponderous books what Homer had known after the Trojan War; that every war ends with a moral headache, with profiteers as in Ithaca and with social unrest as in Nestor's Pylos. This is part of the story, but it is not the story. Teachers, however, disemboweled the stupendous fact of Pierpont Morgan being a banker and Lord Northcliffe being a newspaper man, and were simply overwhelmed by these truisms. Nothing checked their harping on the headache. For two decades they capitalized on the hangover as the veterans did on heroism. Our poor students are the victims of both. They are expected to pay the veterans'

widows some four billion dollars in 1960, and on the other
hand they have to foot the bill for belated teaching, i.e., for
the impoverishment and disempowering of the United States
and the absence of any realistic foreign policy during the last
twenty years. They have to pay exaggerated sums in money
and exaggerated fears in thought.

Now this is certainly a remarkable result for a teacher generation that has honestly tried to give the students the facts
and nothing but the facts. It has insisted that the students
should know what it is all about, beforehand. Yet we see that
the outcome is quite different. The students are not filled
with facts but with terrible forebodings. They fear that propaganda is going to devour them, that profiteers are going to
send them to war, that they will have no jobs. Teachers have
concentrated on facts; students concentrate on expectancies. We
shall see how important this interplay between facts and expectancy is. Here I simply record the fact that the factfinders produced
a fearful generation. They played Hitler's game.

So much for teaching too late. Why do we also learn too
early?

The very essence of learning is to anticipate experience; all
education is life in advance. Simply by being educated persons we anticipate an infinite number of happenings that
would otherwise come to us later, at thirty or fifty or seventy.
Any sensible man of sixty is better fitted to be a judge than
a boy just out of law school. Yet the boy needs his legal
training as a substitute for experience because neither he nor
society has time to wait. So instead of living his own life as
a sequence of "*fiat lux*," as the agenda for the next fifty years,
he gets it as precedents, as facts and acts.

To a certain extent this is obviously normal and right; learning *must* be "too early" as teaching must be "too late." But
it is easy to see how "too early" can become disastrous. We
deal with facts through one organ, with agenda through another. We can enter upon our own happenings only with
faith, love and hope; but we can enter upon the facts simply
by drawing conclusions from them, without actually living.
Our students are to draw their own conclusions from the facts.

That is all to the good as long as blind alleys only are "con-cluded." But if we want to survive, we don't understand the past unless we treat it in terms of the agenda, the things to happen, in our own future. Facts are healthy diet in education only when balanced by "fienda"; things-that-*have*-happened by things-that-*must*-happen. Facts are poison for a person that has not lived through them and has no stomach to do so; they bring life too early into his ken.

Of course we all try to acquire knowledge by buying books and going to lectures. We could not live without anticipating results. The danger sets in when we forget that in so doing we are sharing the speaker's life, the writer's experience. An-ticipation is legitimate as long as we feel deeply about the fact that we live on borrowed life. Then we realize that it is up to us to balance the budget: we cannot live to ourselves, in our own thinking, because we are in debt to others. Thought is begotten by life, and must beget life in turn. Otherwise, when words beget words and books beget reviews "and of making many books there is no end," we get the *"trahison des clercs."* Objectivity without gratitude for the relation of our thought to other people's life blood is intolerable. Our students have no spiritual gratitude; they are told to think for themselves, to become writers, to work out their own salvation —all in flat contradiction to the true relation between living and thinking. And like all heresy, it kills their lives. Degener-ated, they sit on the ruins of Europe as mere sightseers.

Today we break especially the men with the greatest future, the greatest potentialities. We drive them crazy. You all must know cases of students who smelled the good life, yet went to pieces because of the deadlock created for them in college. I once knew the scion of a famous New England family: great-grandfather minister, grandfather college founder, father head of a social settlement in the heart of the coal mines. The boy sought the equivalent for his time. He went to Antioch—where they do practical work, it is true, but in com-plete separation from his studies. He went to Harvard. We became friends. He told me that once in three years had he been allowed to concentrate on one subject for a whole fortnight. A student who at twenty-one had never experienced the blessings of singleness of purpose in his intellectual upbringing! He could not find any service that would have built him up to the rank of his forefathers as a social leader. So he quit Harvard and made a living as the manager of a travelling theater group. He ended up as a speculator in Wall Street. When he came to see me, he looked like a soul in hell and he knew it himself. "I shall try," he said to me when we argued his desertion, "I shall try to jump off the bandwagon of the next boom five minutes ahead of the others. If I can succeed in doing so, I shall recover my self-esteem." Unable to find the long-range faith that had built the lives of three or four former generations, and too sensitive not to search for it, he clung to the short-range substitute for faith—gambling. This man is not perishing because he is less noble than others; on the contrary his is a more real time sense and he is haunted by his conscience which tells him that people like himself must be representative of the future and of the race as a whole.

Second case: the son of a missionary, and among talented brothers himself a powerful mind and a great soul. He has replaced the theological studies of his ancestors by the study of Human Relations and Sociology. But since he cannot believe in anything and especially cannot deny or fight anything with absolute conviction, Hitler, the germ Hitler is in him, day and night, the germ that whispers destruction of the pseudo-life around him, that recommends the big, delivering smash of this whole decadent world. He often feels like going crazy, his big powers being wasted in the separation between his sociological head that classifies everything like a botanist and his living soul and body that must love and hate. Twice he was on the brink of ending his existence. He tries to analyze himself with modern psychology to find out what is wrong. Of course nothing is wrong with him; he is sane in a madhouse. But he is so overcome by his academic environment that he denies himself his own rescue; he could jump to freedom by serving in a more than personal and more than "objective" cause, by serving in loyalty to the living thought that fights destruction through the ages. He has declined such an opportunity because his academic teachers unanimously advised him against interrupting his course of studies. He is soon to be given his Ph.D. in Human Relations for having denied his calling of establishing human relations in the processes of the living Spirit.

In this case, too, we, the academic world, have violated the boy's integrity. He was not by nature a second-rate person who muses about society but one born to carry the sword of the spirit himself, as a knight who thinks for society as its voice and leader. And we told him that no such relation of the individual to society exists, that the mind simply deals with objects, that no roots connect it with the society about which it thinks.

If I had time to go on, I would give you a third equally upsetting case, ending in suicide, another of running away into ship-building, another of a straight A sophomore, brilliant athlete, who quit Harvard for farming, and so the list continues. Some people are matter-of-fact minds with no time sense. Some have a sense for the tangible records of the past, and believe only these; we make these Doubting Thomases of civilization into scholars by the thousand, and give them our best awards. But the most precious men are those who hear the cry from the invisible, smell the corruption around them, and live in the future. These we destroy.

3.   The Antidote to Teaching: Education

The attempt of teachers and students to live on borrowed life is only one instance of a general human trait. Every group or nation tends to follow the line of least resistance marked out by its natural instinct. Thus labor unions continue to ask for shorter hours and higher wages, manufacturers for higher tariffs, railroads for tax exemptions, parties for more political spoils, doctors for longer years of internship, lawyers for more quotations from precedent, ministers for more charity drives and peace meetings. Indeed, we live in a strange society: the individuals are rather self-denying and civilized, often even weary of their power, but the group composed of these anemic individuals lust shamelessly for power.

Now we see why no person or group can safely be left to its natural tendencies. A profession that relies on its natural inertia alone wrecks itself by sheer repetition. The mere production of its special product also generates a poison, like the poisons of muscular fatigue. Theology, medicine, law, unless regenerated by something bigger, are barren. Teaching without something that leads out of the classroom is a blight. When it goes on disemboweling past life it only capitalizes on its privileges within the age; thereby it loses the power for which the privileges were given, the power of guiding the age. All my beloved enemies here, who adapt themselves to the tendencies of the age, all those among us—and we all belong at times to this despondent group—who say, "I certainly have no general philosophy of college education, I fortunately am completely ignorant of the whole in which I occupy one little field"—they all saw off the branch on which their professorship is perched and salaried. What other criterion do they have for their task but the accidental fact that they learned certain methods in their twenties and wish to go on with them and be paid for them as long as possible?

The only thing that can redeem us from our natural inertia is regeneration, the power to make an end and a fresh beginning. This is none other than the Christian faith in death and resurrection. It is not fashionable to say so nowadays, but death alone can guide an age beyond mere living; thought is mere afterthought and must form a cultural lag if it lacks conscious survival of a death situation. Something bigger than ourselves must lift us beyond ourselves. People who eliminate the end of the world from their thinking cannot do anything about the world's resurrection. But this resurrection is our daily task. To die to our habits and prejudices and begin over *in time*; that is the secret of timing, of presence of mind.

The name for the process which regenerates teaching is education: it checks the inertia of both teacher and student. The syllable "e" in education means "out of" and implies movement forward toward something beyond. How often do I go to class with one of my wonderful schemes prepared of ideas and learning; and just as Balaam, I am hired for one thing and commanded to do another; I am compelled by the surge of education to desist from teaching in my prejudiced manner and to alter my course.

Without education a mere teacher must teach too late, because he is unable to stop and change. He remains old furniture of Wuthering Heights, goes on drably instructing in his field or department. I know of a case where a man insisted upon ruining his course by cramming into the last fortnight of his classes an impossible welter of material. I implored him to spare his students this confusion. He insisted that he had offered so many titles and men in the printed catalogue, and that his offer had to be made good. He sold teaching, and declined to educate. He could not say more sadly that he considered himself a hired man. That he ruined twenty potential images of the living God was no concern of his; but the material! the material! that was to be sold for forty-five bucks! And he felt that he did his duty more bravely than I, his tempter.

For the timing of education, or the life of the Word between teacher and student, I would adopt as a motto a famous line of Horace, with a slight change. Who does not agree with his *"vis consilii expers mole ruit sua"*—"a power that does not take counsel collapses from its own weight?" Now our mind, our voice, our doctrines are forces to which the same warning applies. So in behalf of the energy that regenerates correct teaching let us read: "A voice that can only follow its routine, that cannot cut loose from its environment, from the pressure of vested interests, will fall dead and meaningless, and as a blind force it will repeat too late what should no longer be repeated." Our voice must have tasted withdrawal from repetition, must go into the wilderness and take us, teachers and students alike, outside our classroom, our marks and salaries, outside our background and foreground, into the exile of truth. Truth always is found in exile from society. If we call on her in a true ecstasy, a jump outside ourselves, our spirits return purified. Otherwise we fall flat, by the self-centeredness of our professional routine. *Vox consilii expers mole ruit sua* (a voice that does not take counsel collapses from its own weight), and such a voice will bury student with teacher under an avalanche of facts.

The mutual insurance company for capitalizing on the past called teaching, i.e., the company of experts inexperienced in exile, and the mutual exploitation company for getting all the heritage from the past as "1066 and all that," i.e., without the student's own suffering, sympathy, despair, feeling, service, toil —both are detestable. The "too early" and "too cheap" of the student results in two types: the child prodigy and the eternal playboy who has never met his teacher in the exile of truth and who therefore, in his heart, treats all learning as a bit funny. The minds of these eternal children have been reached only by the inertia of the teacher's voice, that academic *Vox consilii expers*. The fruit of such mechanic transmission in the case of the prodigy is a brain flooded with words and verbiage and definitions without the purification of a brainstorm.

4. *The Mennonite Catastrophe of 1939*

The great theme of education is survival: it enables us to out-live, outgrow each stage of life and move on into the next. At present we as teachers are most urgently in need of outgrowing the period of liberal criticism and its common denominator, disbelief. We have not yet recovered from our resentment of denominational narrowness; reminiscences of compulsory chapel, of our parents' and our own experiences with the churches, still color our opinions. Now as long as we rest in disbelief and have not survived it, we are out of step with society. As stowaways from overbearing denominations, we miss the new situation in which the whole of society is thrown today in a vast revolution. Society is out for a gospel regenerated from disbelief; yet we still harp on disbelief as an ultimate. Society will turn against us because it longs for a new continuity of living.

We cannot forego our obligation to testify to this step be-yond disbelief, because otherwise we are apt to cauterize the generative powers of our students. Atheism will form a part of future society, but only as a stage through which each genera-tion passes to a new and fortified belief. The students must be protected from total despair by realizing that their teachers, in their personal lives, have outlived the phase of academic scepticism.

But it is not only the teachers that are at fault. Our whole society has forgotten the means of regeneration which enables both the individual to survive the stages of life and his society to survive succeeding generations. Modern civilization has built on the Reformation principle of universal priesthood, yet today we no longer recognize its supreme importance. A priest is simply an elder, and the elder statesman, the great old man, is the naturally grown priest in any country. His role is superior to that of magistrates because it comes later in the course of life. In Japan, for instance, the elder statesman is the spiritual authority that appoints the acting statesmen.

What is the secret of eldership? It lies in the fact that an old man is through with his own life but not at all through with life. On the contrary, like a grandfather he watches *all* the later generations with a loving wisdom which alone can reconcile their strife. He is the great pacifier, the guardian of life's continuity, because people know that he alone is free from personal or partisan aims. Therefore he is peculiarly the regenerative force in society; he sees to it that the full cycle of life is re-begun in the proper order. And it is the expectation of one day becoming elders that should carry us through the full cycle of our own lives.

It follows from this that the production of leadership, of elders, must take precedence over all social activities. A healthy society indeed requires three distinct functional groups: children and adults as well as elders. Children represent growth; they are trustful, playful, imaginative, creative—the artist is their type. Adults represent professional activity; they work, produce, fight, protect, organize, economize—the fighter, in business or battle, is their most expressive type. But without elders, priests, who embody the secret of survival, the group itself is lost. Producing rugged businessmen and artistic children only, means giving up the survival of the group as such. Therefore no price is too high for the education of men who can rule, teach and pacify, and accordingly educational literature in the past always centered around the nurture of princes and priests and judges.

Now these truths we kept alive in our age by the Amish Men of Pennsylvania, and our own sins are vividly exposed by the stupidity with which their way of life was blocked just a few months ago. If I can succeed in dramatizing this incident, half of my story for tonight will be told.

The Mennonites go back to a declaration of faith in 1632, drawn up in Dort, Holland. In 1690, a Swiss by the name of Jakob Ammon or Amen renewed the sect; from him the conservative wing got its name, Amish Men. They were literal adherents of the principle, "every man a priest," for they had no professional ministry. Everybody had to be a dyed-in-the-wool farmer first, a ruler and a judge later, and at the end the very best acted as preachers. Only the preacher revealed the full power of man's spirit. Hence the younger age-groups were not exposed to an all-devouring intellectual curiosity: they knew there was something to wait for.

There was deep wisdom in all this. The Mennonites perceived the chief aim of education, the production of elders, and they chose the right means: they knew that no mere system of instruction, no set of prescribed "courses" could make true elders, but only a slow growth through all the seasons of man's life on earth. That is why they hurried to make good farmers out of their young men first. They looked at farming with a much deeper insight than the board of trustees of an agricultural college; an unquestionable relation of each member to the soil was the first step toward their highest spiritual office. So they decided that every boy must be an apprentice on a farm in his formative years from eight to twenty; then he would be so well grounded in farming that he could leave it for the next step, when a kind of adult education took him in hand.

But in stepped the sovereign state of Pennsylvania with a new law compelling children to stay in school until 16 or 17 years of age, thereby destroying the basis of the Mennonites' lay ministry. These high school children may become successful commercial farmers, single-crop farmers, land speculators, etc. But they never will be farmers in the sense of a centennial yeomanry, in the sense of an unshakeable foundation for universal priesthood. The frightened Mennonites sent a delegation to the Governor. And he told them: "You behave, or I will pull out your beards." This historic sentence was spoken in 1939 A.D. It signifies the witches' sabbath of scholastic self-adoration. The Amish Men went home red-faced. The proud ones decided to move to Maryland; the wealthy bowed and are going to stay. The group is split. Its spine is broken. The children are driven off into the high school "system."

The very word "system" is perhaps symptomatic of our short-sightedness. If the schools are allowed to form a "system" by themselves as all the rest of our social entities are allowed to do—corporations, professions, unions—we cannot be surprised that they all cease to function as one living universe. Life is no system; it is even less a mere agglomeration of school systems and business systems, all kept apart.

The spiritual history of the Mennonites in Pennsylvania is at an end. Their own governor thought of them only in the terms of an antiquarian. He teased them for daring to break the State's streamlined law, but he was unaware of his own crime: by enforcing the statutory law he broke the laws of human society. The task of producing elders is distinct from the task of producing scientists, businessmen, mechanics, doctors, etc. In an organic society, the training factories for these "jobs" are considered mere makeshifts, which of course will always be needed, but which must take their cue from the laws of biology and mental growth outside themselves. Is it not strange that 2000 years after Christ, 400 years after the Reformation, we should ignore this? Our society does not function because it has thought that the contrast of children and adults is the whole problem. When we degrade the liberal arts college into a prep school for the professions, we have nothing left for educating elders, and without these our country must lose its identity. First things come first.

The Amish Men as a closed group are doomed, yet we need not be sentimental about them if we teachers see the signs of the time and take up the torch where they have been forced to drop it. We too may look to the objectives which give meaning to Kindergarten, High School, College, Graduate School, and Adult Education. These objectives transcend every one of them.

5. Expectancy, the White Magic of Education

Let me sum up the lesson of Pennsylvania thus. Education must include the second half of our lives. For this purpose it must create expectancies in the child that will carry it far. We cannot give "the facts" about the second half because it lies in the future, but we must teach how to reach it with wings unbroken. As the Amish farmer waited for a later period when he could be an elder, so the student must be armed against despair because "arrows of longing" shoot him beyond the stage of scepticism.

The famous psychologist Jung, in Zurich, was flooded with American customers of about forty or fifty. They came to him, he thinks, "in search of a soul" because they had been fed for the first half of their lives with a diet which suits only the second: they had lived on facts, instead of expectancy.

Our colleges today are in the main the outcome of the Enlightenment of 1750, when men were so fascinated with lights, telescopes, clarity—in short, the brave new world of scientific knowledge—that enlightenment seemed an absolute value. But we should know better today, when the era of Enlightenment is ending in brain corrosion, and youth is rebelling to protect its own inner darkness. Yet we go on enlightening at all costs. The students are cauterized before they have grown. And at 45 they give out. They have learned too early; so the specific energies needed in the second half of life are not produced.

The light of expectation for a great and miraculous and surprising future is the only enlightenment that is wholesome. Thinking thrives in the cone of dispersion around expectancy. We cannot learn without repetition, but repetition is insupportable except in this cone of dispersion. Great aspirations make us work and toil with an ease that the "objective" teacher fails to impart. The expectations of our youth must throw us over the hurdle of our fortieth year; it is then that we may find pleasure in facts. Facts are the reverse of the medal; on the obverse side life is a *fiendum,* a "has to come into being."

An education that does not give promises, gives nothing. The declaration of giving facts, and facts only, is a declaration of bankruptcy. Present day teaching, in its false modesty, impresses me as a series of farewell parties to life. True education, however, enables man to survive the limitations and follies of his age and to enter the next; for this reason it tries to endow him with resilience, vision, resources, dreams—and of course forebodings and warnings as well.

Now this is not idealism. It is the most sober approach to teaching; it is right down to brass tacks. I have been the sworn enemy of philosophical idealism all my life because it separates mind and body, spirit and incarnation. I prefer a child to an idea, and Lincoln to any abstract principle.

Is it not a simple fact that a teacher has before him a person whose life has not yet been lived? I have to respect the truth that boys must outgrow the boy, and the man, and the father, and the citizen, and the ruler and the teacher, in due course, and end up as priests and elders. The age of universal priesthood cannot end in the childishness of all without opening a gap for illegitimate elders—dictators and quacks. Once we see that society perishes without true elders, the eternal "too late" of teaching and the eternal "too early" of learning may be brought under our control again: the natural egotisms of teaching adult and precocious child will become subservient to their humble task of timing.

Any society, any person should have as much future as past. The antidote to facts are *"fienda."* The cultural lag represented by teaching, through which society has to assimilate each newcomer, can be balanced by crediting our students with being ancestors of as many generations to come as have gone before. When we look at teaching from the end of man, from the regeneration of the universal order, we shall treat the student as the founder of centuries.

The facts of which we know are so many obstacles to be overcome by providing ourselves stronger than they, yet this strength is not developed by our present way of teaching. It is appalling, for example, to read what modern so-called scientists recommend in marriage. Cowering down under the "law" that man is a product of his environment, they make even marriage a matter of environment, rather than the task of its complete re-creation. They teach it as facts, not as *fienda*. But a marriage that merely conforms to facts, that does not overcome obstacles, is not as inspired as it should be. A new nation, a new people, may be created by a real marriage.

Instead of talking of success and happiness—which are only interesting as long as millions of immigrants represent a continuous belief in a distant future—this continent must now develop, in every one of its children, a faith of *re-immigrating into America.* Today our students, as formerly our immigrants, must be imbued with something far ahead of their "selves." The self takes the line of least resistance. The soldier for the future takes the line of greatest resistance, and only he deserves to be taught because he is the guarantor of our longevity. He alone makes the slack chain that spans past and future taut again.

In this way every familiar fact becomes a vision to the educator. As President Tucker has said, "we must revivify the commonplace." For the truism of yesterday is also the truth of tomorrow, and this it can only become when people are longing for it again and again. They must be made to re-immigrate into the commonplace; and they will do so if we can treat it as the promised land. Even arithmetic can be so treated: the child can be brought with eager anticipation to the fact that two and two are four. Perhaps I am too childish and primitive myself, but the fact that two and two are four really and always still stirs my imagination.

Of course the degree of expectancy we have to develop beforehand varies with the subject matter. For physics it is close to zero; for religion it is infinite. That is why religion cannot be "taught" in a classroom: a soul preparing for infinity is allergic to hourly schedules.

Nobody learns Latin today because nobody expects great things any more from reading Latin texts. To help remedy this, I myself have written a Latin textbook that centers upon rousing great expectancies, but of course I cannot find a publisher for it today, when standardized tests and college board examinations take the place of expectancy.

It is even more difficult to inject the future into political science. To teach the commonplace that a state without justice is gangsterism we must go out of our way. A belief in the possible downfall of civilization is indispensable for its successful defense. A man who does not have insomnia from fear of disintegration will fall asleep when we try to teach him integration. Militia Day was essential to the teaching of justice. The students will have to serve as servants of justice; to fear, not for themselves but for humanity, the terrors of social injustice, and to fight in the war against it. Until they do, they will never understand the Constitution of the United States.

Or consider history. It is taught as though it merely had been. But people tell stories only because we desire to be immersed in the process of how it all came to pass. We do not wish to learn results but to live with the people through the events: by doing so, we ourselves eventuate once more as immigrants, as Americans, as modern men. The function of memory is not to be a museum of inert facts but to keep alive the expectations that are waiting to come true. It should be a cradle out of which grow ancestors, fathers, founders, of generations to come. We remember little more than humiliations and scars unless we are trained in weeding our memory. And that is the purpose of history—it is purified memory as Thucydides said. It should teach us to remember only the things that lie in wait for a denouement in the future.

In this connection it becomes obvious where we fail our students with our curriculum. We answer all kinds of questions for them before they ever have reason to ask the questions themselves, with their whole being. We "introduce" them into everything, in sweeping survey courses and with textbooks that are highly profitable—to the authors. We feed stomachs that are not hungry. And after having spoiled the masses of freshmen, we allow the seniors to fade out as lonely individuals instead of uniting them, as we should, in a great common spiritual experience.

Freshmen should be allowed to grow up to the vital questions that every generation must answer later in an original but corporate effort. Three levels of life each generation has to rediscover. On the lowest level, we treat everything as though it were smaller than the mind which studies it: we regard the world objectively, mechanically, and try to manipulate it as material. At the second level, we deal with human beings on an equal footing, as our brothers and sisters, as part of our own existence: we try to overcome the barriers and differences which separate us and to reach unanimity with these members of our own social body. On the third level, we are overpowered by forces far beyond our individual reach—by devils and angels, famine and revolution, decay or the business cycle: these teach us our own mortality, and lead us to expect death and expect resurrection. Now in the college curriculum the natural sciences represent the level of manipulation, the social sciences the level of unanimity—of vigor, peace, and cooperation—and the humanities the level of death and redirection, survival and overcoming. But in current practice I find the natural sciences more religious and mindful of the two higher levels than the two divisions that should represent them in teaching. That is why we have war and decay.

6. This Extant Moment

We have seen that transformation of the happy child into the successful man into the responsible elder is the condition for the survival of the group. This is the social aspect of the timing of education. It is unsolved today. My attempt to tackle it is always pigeonholed in the different school systems or departments. And naturally so, since it has to attack this very separation, and is justified only in the eyes of persons who fear for the survival of the race. In this seminar I have attempted to enlist your interest in making the liberal arts college the center of timing in a society that has lost this power. Only teachers who have expectancy can give it.

If we do not succeed in rousing expectation, we not only run the risk of producing playboys and cynics; we shall estrange the minorities, the under-privileged, the unemployed, from our society. In that case we cannot hold out against revolution which uses the refuse of society to destroy it. That is why the Civilian Conservation Corps is our great potentiality for saving democracy.

Now leadership for Dartmouth in the CCC also was in sight last winter. I know of course that I as an immigrant am not the man to assume leadership of such a movement. The shepherds of our erring sheep must be Americans. But I think I may act as the shepherd's dog. Since I have pioneered in the rebuilding of industrial and social morale, as founder of the German Work Service, I feel that I can gauge certain mistakes made here in the CCC. As it stands now it is a surface imitation of European models, unreal in its work program, unreal in its existence among the existing communities, uncertain in its significance for society. Being still a relief measure, it neglects the cardinal principle, "equality of service by all." Only the influx of America's gilded youth into the camps would change all this. The CCC should use the student's intellect, the farmer's tenacity, and the city worker's skill, to form a complete model of the regenerative forces in our world. Without *these* standards of living we shall not be able to hold the Western Hemisphere, for we shall not assimilate the lowest stratum of our society.

Well, as the shepherd's dog I have barked and barked. Finally I brought 75 educational advisers of the CCC up here for a week. My plans for reconnecting the college, which is national today, with a national service, were known. Yet I managed, by personal invitation, to get just one out of 200 colleagues into one of the sessions. The camp[3] with which our students were associated during the last year closed down. It was the only camp in which college students did something, at least as far as we know. Probably for that reason bureaucracy clamped down on it. Harvard Press is going to print a book on the theory behind this camp.[4] But now is the time for action. Printing theories has become a device for inaction.

A much brighter view opens up if we turn from the social

[3] Camp William James organized in 1940 in Tunbridge, Vermont.
[4] "Youth and Authority" in *American Youth,* edited by Thacher Winslow and Frank Davidson, Harvard University Press, 1940. Also my first call for armies of industry (1912) is reprinted in this volume.

to the individual aspects of timing in education. The possible insights into this new world are astoundingly rich. One day we shall again learn to connect every change in consciousness with a change in our body or environment, and shall thereby be able to cope with the phasing of teaching much more effectively. The various senses—touch, vision, hearing, smell, taste—will become the special organs for certain periods of growth. We shall know why a boy of 10 should learn by rote, why a boy of 16 must listen to great poetry, why a man of 20 should cultivate his feelings by devoted service in a great cause. Inspiration needs our senses.

The rediscovery of our senses as instruments of the spirit could enable us to outgrow the terrors of our over-visual age. We live far too much on eyesight today; it is dangerous for the cultivation of our feelings. Newsreels and movies destroy our chances for success in the classroom because of their constant irritation of the eye. Homo sapiens is not called sapiens because he sees but because he scents the good life. Common sense is based on smell, not on vision, of the right course. Today we live on common sensations which give a short-lived smell of life. Sensations are perfumed life. The modern hitch-hiker through life pays dearly for sensations because he has lost his smell for the good life.

Well, this program is long. It is far too long for one address. One lecture is no lecture; in human affairs, the single lecture is an abuse. Just as I am wrong in speaking here too late, I am wrong in giving one address. Our modern symposia, forums, conferences, with their five-minute speeches, are caricatures of the life of the mind. As you all know, I usually decline to give just one speech. For many reasons it has become futile. Since the spirit is not the speaker's or the listener's copyright, it takes time to come to any understanding. And modern man has invented the diabolical technique of the single lecture, the mass production of short addresses, to prevent any such deeper understanding. Our scientific gatherings are the final hell of the mind. Any good that might possibly be produced tonight can only result from the whole year that we have gone through together, fighting and hurting each other and seeking each other.

But I will repeat my conviction that the liberal arts college can offer the one thing that may save it in a hostile world, a thing that blind men, professional ambition, progressive education do not give: timing. For timing means freedom from inertia, as Horace expressed it in his *vis concilii expers mole ruit sua*. The timing of mental life is the real life problem of a thinking community, and it will become more and more so because it must cure teaching of being the cultural lag in a restless world. Timing means burying our social pets and predilections in time; it means changing men from a product of spatial environment back to his proper nature as a temporal being.

I am sure, my beloved enemies from all the departments of space, that a hundred years from now, in Erewhon, every school will put in every classroom exact scales for weighing the load of past and the load of future against each other. Every word spoken to 18-year-old boys will be balanced by hours of service so that the boys will feel and expect simultaneously with hearing and seeing.

And on the scales of Erewhon I should be weighed myself, and myself found wanting. For in that land no professor of social philosophy will dare to get up at the end of May and give a talk on a topic that should be dealt with through many winter evenings over many years. And in Erewhon, your President, your Secretary, and the speakers of the evening, after they had committed this high treason against the secrets of timing, would all be hung on high gallows and led through the streets as a warning to any future infringer upon the greatest treasure of humanity—the fullness of its time, the presence of its mind. But let me also hope that some years from now the word spoken out of season tonight may ripen into the maturity of timeliness.

CHAPTER 9

WHEN THE FOUR GOSPELS
WERE WRITTEN

WHEN THE FOUR GOSPELS were written the paths of speech of antiquity were fused. They had met at the crossroad of the crucifixion. The ancient world was at an end. The noon of mankind was established. Our era began.

In our era, the four paths of speech never can lose sight of each other again. Anyone traveling on any of them is saved by the coexistence of the others.

The madness of the magician, the lunacy of the astrologer, the frenzy of the muses, the invisibility of the prophecy had been the limitations of ancient speech. The four paths of speech, ignoring each other deliberately, had become extravagant. In Julius Caesar's days they were dead ends, by their very perfection. Any Greek or Egyptian, Scyth or Israelite, by the very excellency of their speech, became impenetrable and irreconcilable to the other modes by which man also is moved forward into the unknown.

The wailers of the chieftain, the Jeremiads of the impending doom, had uncovered the origins and the final future, for the living. Ancient men had succeeded in hewing out vast avenues of time, back to the hero and forward to the Messiah. Without speech man would have no time, but merely be immersed in time. Animals have no time; they are time's toys. Men conquered time when they began to speak. And they opened the roads towards their own beginnings and towards their own end, from the first dirge to the Jesaian prophecy.

Space too, is not in the animal's possession. The animal is possessed by space. And the man who has not learned to establish heaven and earth is obsessed by space. He remains a fugitive from space, panic-stricken, before he puts the bridle of his orientation, his measurements, on the cosmos. And his orientation required that he should look up to the stars in the sky and invade the firmament with his thoughts so that he might look down, from heaven, from his sky-world, upon the earth. Thus he could settle the earth, downward out of the sky, prescribing place to space, settling the chaotic universe with finite temples. The praisers of the peace between day and night had uncovered the heavens.

And between tribe and tribe, city and city, gods and gods, the Greek poet, the maker, the comparer, the analogist and philosopher, built his reality. The muses could contemplate the multiple world of clans and empires. As Dante's Divine Comedy presupposed the existence of the Church, so Homer presupposed the existence of conflicting bodies politic and opened them to each other. The songs of tragic heroes and cities dramatized the conflicts of men, and so we have admired the ancient wealth of speech.

But these paths of speech could not admit of their presupposition. They had no way of returning to the origin of all speech. We know that times and spaces were mastered by speech, that the living triumphed over death. Speech fulfilled this task of creating times and spaces, but the people who spoke did not know this. They idolized the particular space or the one time relation which was circumscribed by their language. It is as though the devotee of a radio station would deny the necessity or the existence of any other.

Enamoured with their specific way of speech, the people of antiquity mishandled the full task of all speech. The plenitude of speech had to be revealed to the gentiles who had gone astray to the ends of their particular mannerism, and it had to be exerted by Israel who kept this secret of the full truth jealously to herself.

What is the plenitude of speech? Speech in its plenitude forms bodies of time and bodies of space beyond the grave, beyond the moment, beyond the home and the frontier, beyond heaven and earth. Speech conquers all the disintegrations and fissions which abound in nature and of which death is the most drastic form.

The complete unity of all men of all times, from Adam to the last judgement day, would be the greatest expression of our plenitude of speech. And the smallest atom of any living speech would be one hour shared by two people in one spirit regardless of the lapse of time.

Jesus restored to us this plenitude of speech. This was his mission, life, calling, office. He saved the straying gentiles and the locked up Jews. He did this by crossfertilizing the four paths of speech.

He created an eternal unity of spirit from the beginning to the end of history. But he created it by simply speaking to twelve average men. They did not understand that the hour which he spent with them was one hour of eternity which made history. What he said to them made no sense in the frame of reference in which the clansman or the Greek or the Egyptian lived. It made sense only in Israel, which lived in expectation of the end. Even in Israel it made only negative sense in anticipating the kingdom of the Messiah. So Jesus spoke nonsense for the time being. But he undid what people called the time being. For he created a new yardstick for all times. He spoke backwards from the end towards the act of daily life, outside the temple of Solomon.

Jesus reversed the direction of the four paths of speech; he spoke from the end of history towards its beginnings. To this day our era lives by renaissances, rebirths, rediscoveries of ancient civilizations, of buried instincts, origins and prehistoric processes. Jesus began this process. He spoke in the opposite direction from Shaman, Pharaoh, Homer and Moses. The flow of speech in separate riverbeds had led nowhere. Jesus became the Word, the *total* Word beyond the separation and, therefore, he was able to penetrate backwards to the creative starting point *before* the separation. Anybody who wishes to master time and space, who wishes to escape his obsessions, must look to the Noon of our history, the beginning of our era, the appearance of the end, the incarnation of the plenitude of speech, to the total word.

Our contemporaries have neither time nor space. They are the prey of panic. Nomads, rushed, restless, uprooted, they throw their last dollar in the lap of the modern medicine men, astrologers, Greeks and Israelites.

The modern medicine man is the psychologist. He traces everything to origins. The modern astrologer is the investment-banker. He believes in the business cycle. The modern Greeks are all the artists from Beethoven to Picasso. The modern Israelites are the fundamentalists of all descriptions. Whether Roman Catholics or Jehovah's Witnesses, they are convinced that the world deserves to perish.

The man who does not believe that we should throw away our souls for psychology, the business cycle, arts, or orthodoxy, is a Christian.

For he dares to throw himself behind his own words. He dares to feel called, to listen and to respond. His ear is tuned to the end, and he receives his orders from Him who shall be and speaks backward from the end into this present time, so that the present might be redirected from the end. We all are reborn whenever we let a new word change our mind. The total Word is He who showed all men for the first time and forever how to change their minds.

Once the four gospels were written, Jesus' four reversals of the four paths of speech were laid open to inspection for all future generations of men.

In Matthew tribal speech is reversed. The word reaches back to the simplest group's ritual and reverses the sacrificial meal. While a tribe was instituted by slaughtering speechless victims in honor of the dead chieftain's name, in Matthew we hear the victim speak himself into the center of the ritual as giving the name to the whole partaking group.

In Mark astrological or templar speech is reversed. The same Man who challenges us to build one all-inclusive temple out of all of us, as moving stars, is shown to be the first stone of this same temple. If we shall not bury all hopes for all times that men become united in one spirit, we must crystallize around the foundation stone, as the living material, and bring the true heaven to earth, that heaven in which every heart is one star of its firmament.

In Luke prophetical speech is reversed. The Messianic temple is moved from Jerusalem to Rome in the name of him who made his body the temple, who allows the Messianic hope to become real where two or three are gathered in his name. The two or three form the smallest body of time, the minute cell of interlocution, in which there is no fixed father-son, teacher-student, boss-servant relation, but perpetual freedom of each of the members to be now teacher now student, now listener now speaker, now object now subject of the conversation. Where two or three are assembled in the name of the Lord, everybody is willing to be judged with all his shortcomings objectively, everyone is invited to listen to the greetings of affection. Luke establishes the group in which all members may fill the roles of first, second and third person, of speaking mind, listening soul, topical object—all three, thereby become sovereign and superior to any one of these functions. Nobody after Luke can fail to know that kingship and slavery, manhood and womanhood, and mind and body, are now alternatives for any living soul.

And in John artistic or philosophical speech is reversed. The total Word interprets the verbosity of Greek rhetorics. Drunk with words, the Greek mind, whether Homer or Plato, Pindar or Aristotle, was prone to make man the measure. But when God speaks, he creates. And when out of the depth of his silence, Man, the final or real Man, that is the unique one, was called and born, Jesus, all the clever verbosity of the creature mind, of man's mind paled. One Word of God is more powerful than a million words of the Times. He speaks and a man is created. In the beginning was the word, and now the libraries to be written of this one word of God, Jesus, far exceed a billion words of Greek minds. That abstract logic which is allegedly the same for all men, is repudiated: a soul which is fully alive must have her own logic because she is unique. Logic deals with the animal in us, not with the brothers of the *logos*, the "Word," who are irrepeatable, who live once and never again. We owe Jesus our uniqueness.

When the four gospels were written, the crossroads were mapped out in which the four paths of speech had been made to intersect and communicate. And we now need not be carried on these paths of speech any longer as obsessed psychological cases; the spells of pagan speech have vanished. We walk the old paths in the freedom of men who measure them from the goal backward.

Ever since that Noon of the Day of Mankind the paths of speech are used not as one-way streets but with the liberty of those who are free to choose their direction.

CHAPTER 10

TRIBALISM[1]

WE ARE ENTERING NOW A thousand year period in which the rudiments of tribalism will serve us as a refresher course, for the family is destroyed today and speech is destroyed today; and speech and the family are the creations of the tribes. We will stand again at their fountainhead, where they were most intense, because it is there where they were first created. Yet, at this moment, no one understands exactly wherein does lie the claim of tribalism to be regenerated.

The tribe can be defined as an institution to create marriages. Everything about it can be summed up in the one function that it is a family-making institution. The tribe is the *couche*, or the source, of families. The families themselves are transient; the tribe is eternal, the lasting form. One of the greatest errors in most people's thinking today is the illusion that the family into which they have been born was meant to be eternal.

All families must dissolve despite the bad conscience we feel when we cut the apron strings. It can only make havoc and lead to Fascism and racism when it is believed that the family is an aim and purpose in itself. For it is not. When a man comes of age, the family must be second-rate, when we have children, we must give our parents the privilege of being grandparents to them, and that is how they reconquer their family status. Instead, we have the unhappy situation of two parties, one of rugged individualism destroying the family and escaping to the

[1] Part of "Eternal Horizons of Mankind," a lecture course held at Dartmouth College.

West Coast, and the other, the mother party, traveling to army camps and arguing with the corporal about their son's diet. Mothers interfere where they don't belong because few of us know where they do belong. They belong with our children. If parents are not given this chance to become the revered authorities who can redeem our idiotic family life by bringing some spirit of longer history into it an unpurified family life results, with the wife jealous of her mother-in-law and the husband jealous of his father-in-law.

Let me repeat. It is a heresy to say that a family is for eternity. The church may be eternal, but not the family. We need, therefore, permanent institutions to create families, just as we need a spring to supply water and not simply a pond.

We must once again remember that the tribe is the first historical achievement of historical man, and then it will be understood that it isn't the breeding, the animal procreation, which has to be revived today but those thousands of years during which people learned to marry—that is, learned the act of marriage, so that one man and one woman can belong so close together that their children can treat them as one. That act is the historical creation of the first thousand years of humankind, not the breeding which we find in the whole animal kingdom, and which, as animals, we can accept or reject. Tribalism, therefore, is not biological, and belief that it is leads inevitably to mother-worship and ancestor-worship in the most primitive sense. There is nothing wrong with ancestor-worship except that it must be made subservient to the great mission of men to be one throughout all time. Ancestor-worship and marriage are only a first step into the same life we all have to lead, which cannot worship any such flesh, any such purely transient group like the relation between parents and children. I thus have the difficult task of showing you the greatness of the tribes which produced the family, while at the same time, warning you against the superstition that this product of tribalism is in itself something to be worshipped.

The problem of the tribes was to enlighten the act of mating with the *word*. When husband and wife meet, and when the husband stays with his wife through her hour of birth, as Joseph did with Mary, he thereby acquires the right of spiritual authority. When you see that marriage means to go from the blind act of the moment, through the whole life cycle to its most opposite point the childbirth, then you see that the problem of marriage was to alter the course of nature. In nature, animals mate and their young forget who their parents were. They cannot go beyond their individual life cycle, for they do not know what happened before their birth, and they do not know what is going to happen after their death. That we do know this is the essence of history.

To marry means to create *a body of time*. That very wonderful Shakespearian expression is one which we must appropriate for the social sciences. The creation of a body of time is based on being named in the name of the ancestors. Marriages were concluded on the dancing green of the tribe, because they had to be *public*. They were to be entered upon not clandestinely, between you and me, as free lovers think, but under the invocation of the whole group. Marriage was public business, because it meant to force the rest of the tribe to recognize the existence of this newly created special body of time.

All history depends upon the problem that others should know who we are and we should know who others are. We tend to think today that if we do right we haven't to ask anyone else for their permission. That belief is absolutely wrong. Your parents have forced the community to call your mother Mrs. Smith for if they had called her enduringly Miss Brown you would have been born out of wedlock. That people when they marry love each other is not interesting to anybody. But it is very interesting that they have forced the community to say that these people are married. This necessity is hardly realized today, for in the last fifty years we have weakened the rules of the game so completely that it is believed that if two people are in agreement, and they go to a sheriff, somewhere, it is perfectly all right. The result is children's marriages, that are not marriages, because they cannot force upon the community the esteem, the dignity, and the distinction which two people need to have a house of their own, to bring up their children as their own, to bestow upon their children their own name, and to have the authority, for example, to make the religion of their children their own decision.

We still hold to the fiction that parents actually do decide upon the religious upbringing of their children. Of course, in this country, that means the Roman Catholics allow the Church to take over the education of the young, and that the others send their children to Sunday school; or, in other words, parents ask their children to believe in something they themselves do not believe in. We thus have a wonderful arrangement which all comes under the heading: parents have the right to determine the religion of their children.

When marriage was created, that right was understood in a very different sense. The first authority that comes with parenthood is the right to influence, educate and direct one's children, under the one condition that the parents impart their own beliefs to the children. But in ninety per cent of the cases today, parents do not impart their own beliefs. Instead, other institutions, like the churches, or the ethical culture schools, provide beliefs and religion which the parents themselves do not have. Parents have lost the power to demand from the community the authority to bring up the next generation because they have gradually relinquished this authority to the nursery schools, the psychologists, the psychoanalysts or the American Legion. Everyday parents are abdicating their sacred duty to love their children in favor of people who frankly declare that love is damaging.

Marriage is priestly, and cannot be understood without our understanding the meaning of "universal priesthood," the old warcry of the Protestants against the Romans (and which the Romans, by the way, have never denied), that all men are meant to be priests. That belief is one element of the Christian creed that comes directly from the tribes. The first priests instituted in the tribes were mothers and fathers. They were put in authority to represent to the newborn the whole past world of the tribe, by teaching them the sacred names of the tribe, by making these children in their youth form their lips to the invocation of the ancestoral spirit, and by establishing that whenever these names were formed the children had to stand in awe and reverence. The priesthood was the greatest authority under which a human being could be placed—that is, to be allowed to teach others the sacred names of invocation, of prayer and of law.

Parents are there to consecrate their children, and I mean that very literally. For, if we can't consecrate our children, we can't christen them. The two words, "consecrate" and "christen" are the same. To consecrate means to give direction to. Once we teach our children English, we have already separated them from the stem of the human race and made them into Americans, which is very dangerous, because it is a limitation. It is one way among many, and that is why the whole role of Christianity in the matter has been to warn the parents that along with making their children speak Egyptian, Latin, French or English, they have to instill into this limitation, by the Christian first name, the broader message of telling the child: "Yes, you may speak English, but that is not the whole story; you remain a part creature of the whole creation, despite the fact that we allow you now to march along this narrow road of Americanism."

The Christianity of our era simply purifies the old tribal system. The first tribal men, when they allowed parents to consecrate their children, only saw the benefits of giving the children some consecration. When Christianity came into the world, the division between the races, and between the tribes, had reached such a point, that it now seemed important to direct the parents back again—to ask that, although of course, they would teach their children English or Latin or French, would they please inject a warning as well, by giving them biblical names, so that the children would know they do not have to be nationalists. When the biblical names disappeared in Europe around 1900, the World War was the immediate result.

The tribesman wanted to do exactly what people want to do today when they christen their child. He only missed out because he did not know better than to identify his special family group, that is the clan, with the perpetual problem of the child's direction. Whereas Christianity has injected into his family bond the crucial corrective, so that the child knows the limitations of this one tribal connection. No, the first step in history, that parents must bring up their children in the knowledge of what has gone before, this consecration of the child, is the oldest problem of mankind. It is always with us; so much so, that we come to a very practical problem of our day.

Marriage means that father and mother must cooperate spiritually before their child can enter history. In some tribes, that feeling goes so far that the husband actually gets into bed with his wife during the childbirth to share her suffering symbolically. To me, that is one of the sublime rituals of the human race. It is an attempt to convey to the world outside the fact that the father feels as much responsible for the birth of the child as the mother. The full impact of such parental responsibility can best be shown in contrast to the modern system. In ancient times, there was no question that the child was a carrier of the spirit—one to be consecrated, to receive a name, to be understood and to be recognized as a potent member of the group. Therefore, when a malformed or idiotic child was born, it wasn't done as today, when the doctor or nurse must take the responsibility of deciding whether or not to let the newborn baby die. Most of us, fortunately, do not know what is going on in our hospitals. But somebody has to have the responsibility, and today it is the doctor or nurse, with the parents never knowing anything because they are treated like children. It is all over when they come. The wife is in a coma and the husband is having whiskey.

The story of the tribe is that the father must look at the child and take it in his arms and say, "This is my child," as God did when Jesus was baptized in the river Jordan, "He is my child in whom I take pleasure." This formula is very ancient because in the spiritual ancestry of man, a child was to be received into the spiritual world, just as it is received from the womb into the physical world. All of these rituals have been forgotten by those who believe in living simply by Nature, or by Motherhood, or by J. J. Rousseau or Benjamin Franklin, those half-baked people who think that life is natural. Nothing in our lives is natural; everything is spiritual. By speaking we enter into the great lifestream of humanity from beginning to end, and somebody has had to impart this lifestream to us. Just as a mother imparts life to the body, so a father imparts life by receiving and naming his child, and that is spiritual.

That the father would again have the responsibility of saying yes or no to the child would be the first rediscovery of tribalism in our age. This system may seem very cruel, because most people think that every child born should live. Of course, it should; but we mistake the situation if we ignore the fact that somebody has to say, "This is a full-fledged human being." For, when a child is born with three heads and four legs a decision has to be made: "Should he live?" He who decides this, is the father; he becomes the father in the act. That people are made to live so, without anybody deciding this, is a scandal, and nothing but brutality. Yet, it is thought that such have to be, because we have completely cowtowed to what we call Nature. Our whole picture of humanity has been falsified because everyone thinks we should be one with nature. It would be much better if we would be one with the human race, which is a living creature in its process of revelation! Humanity has the great task of staying one through all times. The human animal is that animal which is ubiquitous and always and which can acquire the consciousness of everywhereness and all-the-timeness. No elephant knows what went on before him and what will come after him and no animal knows what happens next door around the corner. We can, aye, we must! Man is extending all the time his space and his time and creating super-sensual periods and supersensual spaces. Marriage allows him to do this because it makes it possible for children to know of ancestors.

Father and mother represent to the child, in the absence of the tribal meeting for the first twenty years of his life, the existence of this big entity, the tribe. The child is not taken to the assemblies of the grown-ups, but is informed in the same way that education told us of the United Nations, and America, and private property and the law, though we lived in our homes innocently. The father and mother are the local priests who testify to the child of the existence of a wider world and of a wider reality. How is this done? In the family group, there are always several youngsters growing up under the care of the parents and receiving from them, as the first thing, the knowledge that they share their mother tongue, or, as in the tribe, the father tongue—in the law of the jungle, the male speaks, and a child must learn his father's tongue. The father, and in the father's absence, the mother, represents the tribe to the children. All the families, therefore, must have direct access to the source of their existence, the center of the tribe, and this is achieved through the meeting ground. At the tribal meeting, such decisions are made as those for the funeral of a warrior, for the warpath against the enemy, and for the expiation of deviations from tribal behavior. In the case of marriages, the meeting and decision-making we call an orgy, because it had to be danced. These wild dances in public of the marriageable people sealed them, so to speak, as future fathers and mothers in the tribe. In the tremendous upheaval of the wedding, the parents became the carriers of the tribal law. They are endowed with the spirit which has led to the use of the word *Ehe* to mean in German both law and marriage. Marriage was thus the carrier of the law, the priesthood by which the parents represent the law of the tribe. In the ancient languages, law and marriage are very often the same word, for it meant the same thing to get married and to become the legislator or the representative of the law.

In any marriage, the whole tribal law became documented, for it was written on the skin of the married people in the form of the tattoo. Tattoo is the first writing of the tribe. The constitution of the tribe, that authority of the tribe which can be invoked, is painted and depicted in the tattoo. We must come to understand that the tattoo is not a superstition or something funny, but that in the tattoo of the modern sailor, we have the last remnant of the first layer of script. It is simply not true that writing was invented by the Egyptians, or that the Greeks inherited script from the Phoenicians, and so on. It is much more complicated. The tribe writes, too, but it writes on living bodies. It hasn't anything more permanent, because the tribe moves; so the best they could do was to write the law of the tribe on the skin of the people who are ready to marry. They then bring the tribal law everywhere with them. Each married member of the tribe is a single document, one edition of the constitution. In these orgies, therefore, there were very painful operations. In order to get married, these people had to undergo, perhaps, circumcision and incisions; their noses were made to stand out, and so on, and in some tribes, there was trepanation, the perforation of the skullbone, something we do now to get rid of blood clots in the brain. The tribal man had all kinds of ways of making pain the great memorizer. As is well known, tattoos are not easy. They are usually burned into the skin; but, whatever the methods by which the tattoos were inflicted on these poor people, it is only one form. We can still see today in some African tribes, people with distorted ear lobes or lips, evidences of the extreme hardships connected with the moment of making the child of nature into the bearer of the law of history.

In the orgies of the meeting ground, people of accidental origin are made into members of one group. They are all identified by the same tattoo, and are then recognized by the same constitution. An order is imposed on their living, because by the tattoo it is said whom you can marry and whom you can't marry. Thus, the tattoo is also a taboo. One's tattoo shows that he cannot marry those who have exactly the same tattoo, and in that way, inbreeding is excluded. The great thing about the tribe is that it created orderly marriage, and for this purpose, it had to invent "incest." What is incest?

Incest is the destruction of a sacred space inside of which the passions of sex shall not rage. All modern people show the weakening of the traditions of the tribe by the writing of poetry or drama on incest. They especially now seem to harp on the love between brother and sister and on the Oedipus complex. These writings show us that it is high time to study the tribe again, because the tribe is the institution that has outlawed incest. In nature, there is no such law. Animals do inbreed if you leave them to themselves. Chastity has nothing to do with morality in the sense of evil thinking. Chastity is the creation of a spare room inside of which man is *unafraid of the other sex.* What we call a home today is first of all a relationship between the members of the family such that they cannot intermarry nor have to fear being raped. Parents and children to each other form one body of time, and the consecration of the children makes it necessary that the father and mother remain to these children, father and mother. It is no small matter, and quite unnatural, that for the last 8000 years parents have not slept with their children. A father would love to sleep with his daughter because she is very young and beautiful. But it is not done because he loves her too much and his love outweighs his desire. For all the sneering at history which goes on today, and for all the ridiculing of religion, most of us continue to believe that one's daughter is sacred to the father; and to believe that, is to be part of the greatest historical tradition. We recognize in our daughter someone who must reach the future in freedom.

Chastity is then the creation or the division of the world of men into two spaces: one for sex, and the other for non-sex. That is, the orgies in the meeting ground, and the brotherhood or the sisterhood of the home are correlated. We can say that the tribe increases the frenzy while they meet in orgy and allows all sorts of sexual libertinage, and licentiousness, in order to better sanctify and consecrate the private groups, the small groups inside of which what happens at the orgy must be completely excluded, to be not even thought of. A brother does not think of his sister as a sexual being, and a sister should not think of a brother as a sexual being. Mothers should not think of their sons as being good to sleep with and fathers should not of their daughters. We have to learn this lesson again because it is the root of all human purity.

We all have to know that men have in themselves this tremendous starting point of orientation, that there has to be with human beings two worlds, one in which the consecration, the sanctuary of the spirit of speech, of naming each other, is so strong that the physical has no rights; and the other where the spirit is not there, where the physical pleasure in another human's body prevails. If a young man does not make this distinction, the girl to whom he is going to propose will find out. If he only runs after her for her fair looks or for her impertinence or for her sensuousness, and if she is any good, she will recognize that he has not the other power in himself to create, at random, the second step, into the sanctuary. A man has to have a sister and a bride in his heart before he can get married. If he is only expelling the sister or the mother by this woman, he can get a strumpet, but not a wife. And names have nothing to do with it, for one can get married and still have a strumpet for a wife. It is up to a young man to let his sweetheart know that he knows the other world of non-sex. If he does not know both worlds he cannot get married. That is the difference between puberty and the power to get married. Our physical potency is one thing; and our potency to consecrate is another; the tribe has introduced this balance of power within us, so that we can recreate the sanctuary inside of which there is chastity; the tribe is this balance!

As I have said, chastity has nothing to do with our physical being, but it is our power of the spirit in favor of the whole human race to abdicate for the time being from our physical urge. I have heard people say that they cannot vow chastity as a monk and heard many people declaim that the celibacy of priesthood is unnatural and that there should be no celibacy. But as long as men live as they do, there have to be monks and nuns to remind us that we too have the power of celibacy at random. All of these special institutions today of the monk and the nun, that is of the eternal virgin, are only reminders to the normal being that he has this power of priesthood inside of him. What is a priest? A man who can throw the switch between his physical wave length, which goes from twenty to sixty, in which we want to procreate, and his historical role in which he stands for the direction of the whole human race through hundreds and thousands of years. There is nothing abstract in what I am calling the spirit here. When we say to somebody "sister," we place her in the timestream of thousands of years. When we say to someone "sweetheart," we want to have her and kiss her right now. And therefore, in our sister we face eternity, and in our sweetheart we face the moment.

Everyone knows these great secrets and I am trying only to add consciousness and some respect for them. For it is unimportant today whether people go to church or not, because everyone misunderstands the church anyway, but it is terribly important that people should rediscover their divinity in this power to be alternatingly a lover and a brother. It is the sovereignty of man, that by the simple word "sister," he can suddenly see in his sweetheart a human being who is not dependent on his lust. The great story of the birth of Jesus is that the whole question of marriage as it was handled in the tribe, is in the story of the Virgin Birth put on just the opposite pole, where there is no lust and no relation of sensuousness. When the child was born, Joseph acted out the role of the midwife, because Mary had become his sister. And that is the most interesting part of the Virgin Birth, that Joseph and Mary were brother and sister. This principle runs through all humanity. But today, with the aid of the psychoanalyst, it is nearly lost, because people are told that even the mother is an object of lust. It is perfectly true that in the animal kingdom mothers and fathers after a short while do not exist. When an animal is in heat, consciousness is concentrated so totally on copulation that nothing else matters. There is no horizon.

Perhaps we may use the word "horizon" with some lasting effect. The tribe established horizons of time and space over its members. The horizon places even the greatest passion, the passion of sex, in the realm of permanency. When the sun rises on our passion, it is very hard to set the sunset on the opposite horizon, namely the mother giving birth to the child, for by then our passion has completely died down, and we want to look in the other direction. It is not agreeable to see a birth. It is travail and it is work and no one wants to see it. Now the horizon of the tribe establishes the identity between the sunrise and the sunset of our passion, and it teaches us that after the sunset there is a sunrise again. This first calendar of human life tried to identify passion and non-passion, ecstasy and indifference. Most everybody today is trying to be cold only, or objective. Our pre-ancestors in this country tried in their revivals to be ecstatic. But the problem is to be the same person in both ecstasy and indifference, each being a side of life. Nobody can be either simply objective or passionate. Historical life only begins when we can remind ourselves in the moment of passion that there will be a sunset to the passion, and then we can remember in our moment of indifference that there has been a consecration of the past which now enables us to stick, despite our indifference, to the wife of our choosing.

Long ago, St. Augustine, the bishop of Hippo, and a Father of the Church, was asked the question: "Why not incest? Isn't it very handy?" And he said that it was forbidden for a simple reason. Whenever a name of love has been given already to a sister or mother, or in those days even an aunt or cousin, we cannot approach this person with a new name. Love needs a name given to this sweetheart or bride for the first time. Incest is every situation in which somebody has first been called by a dispassionate name like sister and is then approached with the new name of passionate love. Love must give a person a name as though we saw them for the first time; and since between mothers and sisters, brothers and fathers, there exists already one name of love, the second name would be impaired. Whenever we have already given a name of no-passion, like sister, we can never approach the situation in the way it should be approached. Therefore, in the orgies that we spoke of earlier, the meeting between man and woman was enveloped in ecstasy as though they had really never seen each other before. In addition, the tribes were very carefully split into marriage groups. The tribe had sub-divisions, usually signified by their particular totem; one had the fish on the totem, one the eagle, a third the raven or the wolf, and so on. These totemic divisions have the profound reason that it prevented marriageable people from meeting without ecstasy.

Today the incest problem is not, as we all know, a physical problem inside the family. No one really thinks of marrying his sister, but by marrying the girl with whom we went to school from our eighth to thirteenth year, we may already be making a mistake, because we have first called her as a fellow child, and as a classmate and a playmate, and such a prior relationship is not the true origin of marriage. I feel that the problem of inbreeding is very much one of the schools and not so much of the family. In marriage, the sequence is: first you see the girl as somebody whom you desire, and then you add the horizon of her becoming a sister, and the mother of your children and the daughter of your parents. If we pervert this sequence, we stand things on their head, because passion is the founding element, and objectivity or realism, as we like to call it, or factualism, is always that which comes later. So, I think that St. Augustine's answer is very beautiful. He said that whenever a name of love has been borrowed by the younger generation from the parents,—we call someone sister or mother because we were taught by our parents to use these terms—we are lukewarm because our feeling is hereditary. Inherited love, therefore, is the reason for the incest rule, because if we have already lived with these people in affection, but without passion, they cannot become the object of passion. St. Augustine's statement solves many riddles, and it is the only explanation I have found in the literature on this subject which holds water, which is really completely correct. Physically, we can never really decide these matters but we can very well ask our tongue. When our tongue has already applied a name within the family relation, we shall hardly be able to use the name for the beloved as though this was for the first time. The subdivisions of the tribe try to pay attention to this problem of keeping the women whom the tribesmen encounter on the meeting ground as yet unnamed. If you have never spoken to the girl before, and you speak to her for the first time, there is the great experience of giving someone for the first time her name so totally that there is nothing you have to obliterate; it is really new to you. Later, she can become old and familiar to you, but at that great hour, she is somebody entering your horizon for the first time. This is called "introduction" and is a mighty event.

Now, about the tribal totems, let me say something that may illustrate how they are really a spiritual or inspiring part of human living. Once, when I was hiking in British Columbia, I was struck with a realization that I have never found in any books. We were traveling in unexplored country, without maps, and it was necessary there to walk through the underbrush on the paths made by the great animals, like the elk or the moose. We didn't know where we were going, and when we found these paths made by the animals, we were extremely grateful. Now the meeting grounds of the weak, frail primitive men were the paths created by the animals. And the animal totem is, I am quite convinced, not only the superstition that man is descended from the eagle or from the bear, as most textbooks tell us, but it is the simple acknowledgment of spiritual gratitude to the animals for the organization they provided. The incredibly weak man of that time, who had no iron axe or steel weapon, and who would have had to fell trees to find a place of union inside the jungle, was helped considerably by these animals. So man, in not only giving a name to his ancestors, but also in naming himself after the animals, recognized his dependency on the universe, on the existing cosmic order. We have for thousands of years, and even modern man is included, followed the paths of the created world. The first five days of creation are much more with modern man than he cares to admit when he lives in urbanized cities. Few of us see the extent to which we still follow today the water courses, and the animal courses and even the bird's directness. All of the animals which we find used in the totems of the tribes have in some way or another actually directed the paths of men on this earth.

The word "path" we should make the foundation of our political understanding of tribalism. The tribes tried to find paths in the jungle, paths in time, paths in the thicket, and that is why going upstream following the watercourses, or following the paths of the wild animals, was the first political power that enabled these groups to become a little larger than the small group of husband, wife and children. The relation of the tribesman to the animals is one of spiritual gratitude for their directing powers, for the work done for them, because the elephant, the lion and the fox, etc., were superior to men. This understanding will also explain all the strange ideas in the Old Testament and in antiquity about dragons and sphinxes and cherubs. People felt that man should base his existence on the bringing together of all the achievements of the animal kingdom and putting them to use. Thus, man's relation to the animals has nothing to do with his pedigree in the physical sense, but it has a great deal to do with his devotion to what existed already, to the organization of the world which he was free to inherit. I think that most people today are unaware of, and the textbooks don't even mention, this confrontation of primitive man with the achievements of the animals. They think that man evolved out of the animals. I think that is of no interest to anyone. Whether or not we came from the apes is a very minor matter compared to the great question of how much use primitive man made out of what the animals already did. We are then examining a much different relation—one of working together, and one of primitive man owing the animals something. This will explain the sacredness in which the animal world was held.

We can see now that not only does the tribe produce marriage, but our whole understanding of tribalism—tattoo, totem, incest rules and taboo, all of these, all of these strange and wonderful practices—all go back to the one simple, central problem: How do two people so fall in love, that their marriage means more than the satisfaction of their momentary lust?

CHAPTER 11

POLYBIUS, OR THE

REPRODUCTION OF GOVERNMENT[1]

Rotation of Government

BETWEEN 1517 AND 1918 FOUR great forms of government arose which entrusted the regeneration of society to the laymen, to a secular power. All these revolutions stand for a sovereignty of the temporal. The secular mind is made the sovereign, possessing in its own right the knowledge of good and evil. The layman, the commoner, the individual, the cog in the machine—everybody may now understand government. The secrets of the State are laid open to the public, step by step. The four great forms of government all have one and the same passion: to be free from the visible Catholic Church. But they also have many other things in common. By comparing them we shall get the best available material for a real political science of mankind. We can then present to the political scientist certain statements which are more than mere abstract definitions of our own.

First of all, these forms of government are the well-known, ancient forms described by Aristotle: monarchy, aristocracy, democracy, and dictatorship. Monarchy, as the hereditary form of government; aristocracy, as the system of co-optation; and democracy, as that of election, are represented by Germany, England and France respectively. And Russia ended the series by returning to the most comprehensive form, dictatorship.

[1] From *Out of Revolution, Autobiography of Western Man*, pp. 453–482. Originally published by Morrow, 1938. Third Edition published 1969 by Argo Books.

Secondly, these forms of government follow each other in order, but not within the same country. Once they have appeared, each in its own country and in its proper order, they co-exist. Kings, parliaments, capitalists and proletariats rule simultaneously.

Thirdly, the European countries form a unity in spite of their plurality. By acting as independent revolutionary bodies, they have achieved something in common, and each has achieved something for all. The European concert is a fact, not a dream. It goes deeper than a mere concert of ministers or presidents. It is a common campaign for the best form of government.

Fourthly, the ancients knew the rotation of constitutions. Polybius described it in detail, telling how every form of government degenerated and thereby failed, not because of its wrong measures but because it fell into the hands of the wrong men. Polybius and Aristotle were considered classics on this topic of the wheel of political fortune.[1] But nobody ever asked, during the Christian Era, whether the classical statement could be tested by the experience of Christian nations. There was a good reason for this neglect of so natural a question. Christians, knowing all the failures of paganism, hated to think of such an unreasonable rotation: the world was redeemed from the curse of blind repetition.

Today, Christians are much more modest; they make no distinction between antiquity and the Christian era. Few people can answer the very moderate question: "Is there any difference between the Christian era and antiquity?" Many would say, offhand, in a pessimistic tone: "None whatever." After all, Christians even kept slavery among their legal and constitutional forms until 1865. How, then, is there any difference? Christianity is a beautiful ritual which we observe on Sundays; but a Christian era does not exist.

We do not share this conviction. The Christian era has established something which is completely outside the Sunday ritual and yet is universal, something quite simple, and yet miraculous. Aristotle and Polybius were right in their day;

[1] Polybius, VI, 3 ff.; Aristotle, *Politics*, VIII, 5, 12.

their pessimistic outlook for a permanent rotation of governments and constitutions was justified; the forms of government were mortal and transient. But the Christian era has achieved something very different from the pagans, with their undeniable law of mortality. It has not been content with the rotation of monarchy, aristocracy, democracy and dictatorship; it has made them coexist. The coexistence of these four political forms in one world is not a bare coexistence; it means the inter-penetration of each one with all the rest. The abuses of one form of government, at the circumference of its sphere of influence, led to reaction. Since Germany's party of religion does not exist in England, the King of England must step down and become the first gentleman of his kingdom. Since the English type of Commonwealth does not exist in France, the aristocrats must step down and become the *élite* in a republic. Since the French variety of capital does not exist in Russia, capital must step down and become one social force among many.

Thus, regeneration occurs not at the centre but at the outer fringe. Through this happy kind of safety-valve, the centre of each form of government remains for centuries without change. The coexistence of different countries obviates the crude rotation of antiquity. The peoples co-operate and co-exist, not merely geographically or mechanically, but morally, as one collective system of interplay and mutual dependence.

This mutual dependence, by its very nature, is opposed to the domination or subjection of one country by another. It is revealed best in times where the motherland of one form is most deeply humiliated in its power abroad. Never was France more successful in urging national unity and indissolubility upon her neighbors, Italy and Germany, than in the period of Napoleon III, when she was at the lowest ebb of internal debasement and oppression. It was as though the Italians and Germans—and the English, too—could only be completely bewitched by the Gospel of 1789 when it no longer carried any notion of French superiority, as it had in the days of the first Napoleon.

English parliamentarism made its way to the Continent at

the time of the loss of its first empire. In the days of England's greatest distress the rules of the House of Commons, hitherto kept secret, were revealed to the Colonies in America and to the Continent of Europe. The House of Commons became the Mother of Parliaments in the dark hour when habeas corpus and free speech were suspended at home. Then it was that all the English parliamentary expressions became the public property of the civilized world. The efficient civil service of the Lutheran monarchy was not copied by France until the Thirty Years' War, under Richelieu and Mazarin, i.e., at the low ebb of the German Reformation.

All these forms of government were first brought forward by a tremendous and formidable explosion. Protestanism, Common Law, Constitutionalism, Sovietism, first tried the way of loud, noisy and belligerent expansion. The Huguenots, the Fronde, Napoleon, the Catalonians, the Bolsheviks, all are types of violent expansion; each belongs to the first chapter of a World Revolution. But they all reached their limit very soon. None of these forms of government was allowed to carry the day completely. Each revolution had to settle down in a particular European area; it had to occupy one certain part of the earth's surface. And this part of the world was given its very shape by the fact of its undergoing the immediate influence of one of the World Revolutions. Neither the German nor the English nor the French nor the Russian nation existed in its modern form before the specific revolution which centred within its borders.

England had no unity with Ireland and Scotland; France had not assimilated Alsace or Provence; Russia had contained the Western Catholic and Protestant territories; and Germany had embraced Switzerland and the Netherlands, before the split of Religious Parties determined the new boundary of the German nation. No Great Power in Europe has ever successfully incorporated a territory into its frontiers unless that territory has shared the uniting, spiritual experience of its revolution.

Alsace is in the peculiar position of having lived through the Reformation with the German, through the French Revolution with the French. It went through the German Reformation from beginning to end (1517–1555 and 1618–1654), and by this experience it was incorporated into the German nation. It cannot be compared with Switzerland, which left the Empire before the Reformation in 1499. Later, in its French days, the expulsion of the Huguenots was not extended to the Alsatian Protestants. On the other hand, it was in Alsace, which had been governed by the French King since 1680, that the *Marseillaise* was composed by Rouget de Lisle. Alsatian soldiers were in the forefront of the Napoleonic wars, and Marshal Ney hailed from Saarlouis.

The Alsatians have lived through two different World Revolutions. Under German rulers they maintained their French ideas of citizenship born of 1789, and now, under French government, they are again standing for the old German liberties of the Reformation. They are, necessarily, the famous *Hans im Schnakeloch*, of whom the Alsatian popular song runs:

> "Johnny in the midge's hole
>   Has everything his heart could wish—
> And what he has he does not want,
>   And what he wants he does not have.
> Johnny in the midge's hole
>   Has everything his heart could wish. . . ."

The World Revolutions all start without reference to space, with an absolute programme for the whole of mankind, and a vision of a new earth. They all believe themselves to be the vessel of eternal, revealed, definite truth. Only reluctantly do they come back to the old earth. Every revolution makes the painful discovery that it is geographically conditioned. Nothing seems more insulting to its great leaders and great minds than to be reminded of the earthly premises on which their conclusions rest. The history of the first revolutionary period is nothing but this process of reluctant habitation, taking root in a particular soil.

In Russia we have the spectacle of an international revolution turning national before our very eyes. But France was limited in the same way by the restoration of her frontiers

of 1792 in 1815. The European scope of the British Commonwealth had to be made clear to the English Parliament by William III. In return for their liberties on the seven seas, they
had to pay the full price, guaranteeing their European neigh-
bour, the Netherlands, and participating in the wars against
Louis XIV on the Continent as allies of the Catholic Emperor.
The British Parliament even endured the Hanoverians, although they remained absolute monarchs on the Continent. In
other words, 1688 ended the possibility of splendid isolation
for the English gentry. This was the *conditio sine qua non* of
William's accession. The end of a revolution comes when it
ceases to believe in its own universality—when its natural hope
of expansion is given up. This is what happened in 1555, when
the opposition to the pope had to recognize that no universal
reformation of the Church was possible. It was in the Peace
of Religion of 1555 that the individual territory was made the
battlefield of reform.

What the fanatical first period, with all its noise and tumult
can never do, is accomplished during the period of humilia-
tion. Only then do the forms of the revolution become arti-
cles of export which find willing buyers in other nations; for
only then can a neighbour-state take the same free attitude
which was the mainspring of the revolution in its motherland.

All great revolutions presuppose a colossal effort of human
liberty and free will. They all arrive at their limits because
they underestimate the freedom of their neighbours. The
Great Revolutions never take into account the fact that mankind cannot act all at once. They overestimate the capacity
of humanity for simultaneous change. They are bound to do
so, because they appeal to only one class of mankind.

Every class has, no doubt about that, a common interest
all over the world. High Magistrates, gentlemen, bourgeois,
and proletarians are all international classes. Marx's mistake
was that he believed in only two classes, capitalists and proletarians. In actual fact, land-owners and rulers have opposing
interests; and Fascism has been successful in opposing Marxism
because it has rediscovered the existence of two types of men

who are neither capitalists nor proletarians. The type of Magistrate, judge, politician, officer, and the type of sailor or farmer had fought their battles against popes and kings long before Labour arrayed itself against Capital.

"Love Thine Enemy" in Politics

Our first observation in this chapter was that the Polybian rotation of the forms of government was changed in the Christian era into a coexistence of all these forms in one civilization. This fact throws a crosslight on Marxism, which completely neglected the Christian element of contemporaneity between antagonists. In politics "love thy enemy" means that we must learn to bear the existence of a conflicting form of government. All these forms of government survive thanks to the faith and belief of their supporters. And the rationalist, who believes in a certain best form of government, cannot help feeling that this threatens his most sacred principles. The more realistic political scientists have gone to the opposite extreme and made government the empirical product of soil, earth, history, climate, environment.

We can adhere neither to the idealists, the best-government dogmatists, nor to the geographical, nationalistic school. Both theories would split humanity into meaningless atoms. He who is interested only in the "best" form of government cuts all ties between the different phases through which political institutions have passed; he destroys all respect and reverence for continuity. And, on the other hand, the admirer of England's or Andorra's romantic peculiarities cuts across our loyalties to a world-wide order. Man can neither bear to be cut off from his roots in the past, nor to have all his highest beliefs confined within the bounds of one nation or continent. The results of our survey go against both; against the destroyer of continuity and the destroyer of our unity in space. For all these revolutions attempted the same great thing, at different times and with different means, but for exactly the same purpose!

All of them faced a disintegration of the type of man who was produced by society. All of them were haunted by a worthless, slavish, dwarfish order of things. All thought of man as the image of God. The Bolsheviks would not take so much trouble to be godless if they did not feel godlike themselves. Each of these revolutions could have cried with Nietzsche: "If God exists, how can I bear not to be God?"

Each revolution, originating at the circumference of a preceding revolution, faced the eternal dilemma of a divine and a bestial nature in man. Each entrusted the solution of this dilemma to a different class, that is, to:

> Nobility
> Gentry
> Bourgeoisie
> Proletariat

In each of these classes, despair over the past and hope for the future kindled the spark of passionate love for a world reborn. The bearers of the gospel of man as the Son of God, and of nations as the nurseries of the sons of God, scorned the caricatures of humanity whom they met in real life. These men found in the monasteries of Saxony, at the Court of St. James, at Versailles or St. Petersburg, were too clearly sons of man, ay, of cattle. They had forfeited their share of divinity and inspiration.

This caricature of the former man or type was called "capitalist" by Marx, "aristocrat" by Robespierre, "tyrant" or "despot" by Pym, and the "Antichrist" or the "Whore of Babylon" by Luther. And the Nazis call the proletarian "underman," "*tchandala*," in order to demolish him. Thus we get a list of aggressive names, contrasting vividly with our own sober and prosaic sequence:

	Whore of Babylon
	Antichrist
Nobility	Tyrant
Gentry	Aristocrat
Bourgeoisie	Capitalist
Proletariat	Underman

The torchbearers of a new revolution push out the degraded type and set about creating a new, unheard-of race. For that purpose cold, descriptive names would have been useless.

The new sovereign of France had to be a self-made man and was proclaimed a citizen. The new sovereigns of Great Britain became Commoners and Christian gentlemen. The Prince, still a monster in 1515, in Machiavelli's *Principe*, was elevated by Luther in the years after 1517 to the respectable position of a High Magistrate. And today the workers, rough and ready, have been turned into proletarians, the distinguished first members of a classless society.

Propaganda Title	Descriptive Name	Swear-word
. . . .	Pope	Anti-Christ
High Magistrate	Prince	Tyrant
Christian Gentleman	Noble	Aristocrat
		Tory
Citizen	Bourgeois	Capitalist
Proletarian	Worker	(Underman)

It reads, left and right, like obverse and reverse of a medal, the medal itself in reality embracing both sides.

But the list is not complete. The propaganda title of the pope is lacking. The slanderous name for the proletarian is doubtful too, because it is not used by a subsequent post-proletarian revolution, but by the defenders of the pre-Marxian order of things; in other words, by the counter-revolutionaries.

Thus the two corners of the picture, beginning and end, cannot be defined on the basis of the investigations put before the reader in this first part. Fascism and papacy—the present-day reaction against Communism in the form of black, blue, silver and brown shirts, and the existence of a Catholic Church in Europe and America—are left unexplained. Yet they are sovereign powers for the modern masses; and they turn people into friends or enemies with all possible thoroughness.

Al Smith could not become President of the United States because he was Catholic. Fascism could not succeed in Italy until it made peace with the papacy. It works both ways, but it works. And the reproduction of mankind in the Christian world depends on the relative power or weakness of these elements. Italy, Rome, Florence, Venice, Vienna, have not been mentioned in the preceding chapters. Fascism and papacy are both at home in Italy. Our excavations in the revolutionary lava have unlocked the geological secrets of English and German religious language and of the capitalistic and proletarian vernacular; but we must turn to Italy if we wish to understand the liberties of the Roman Church and the aspirations and prospects of Fascism.

But the results reached here will also give a new and better interpretation of the modern revolutions. Their very essence was, as we found, to be universal and totalitarian without being unique. One coexisted with all the rest, and that was the chief feature of modern civilization which gave it the right to bear the name European.

The coexistence of imperialism and clericalism, with the four modern forms of temporal power, changes the picture once more. The laws for the future of mankind, resulting from its past, can only be discovered after we have deepened our perspective.

Marching in Echelon

Still, the results of our investigations already offer some hints for further research. First of all, the rotation of the forms of government from monarchy through aristocracy and from democracy to dictatorship is an advance from small territories to large.

The average State of the Reformation was a small fraction of the area covered by Cromwell's first Commonwealth. Again, the Continental mass of France is much greater than that of the British Isles. And Russia is obviously a territorial problem in itself, with forty times as great an area and six times as many people as France had in 1789.

1517 Individual *State*, Saxony for instance. Average size that of Rhode Island to that of Yorkshire, with half a million people.

1649 British Commonwealth and British Sea. Eight million people.
1789 Natural frontiers of the French *Nation*, including all parts of Caesar's Gaul (Belgium, Rhineland); it would exceed modern France, and in its area in 1789 there probably lived 32,000,000 people.
1917 Eurasia U.S.S.R. 150,000,000 people in an area forty times as big as modern France.

Confusion had reigned in Germany at the beginning of the Reformation. Every knight, every valley, every township and municipality had undertaken its reforms separately. The wars against Hutten and Sickingen (in 1523) and the Peasants' War (in 1525) were the cruel answer to this foreshortening of the picture. It was the whole of each German territory with its forests, and not merely one village or city, that had to be organized by the Lutheran High Magistrate.

The British aristocracy of 1649 attacked a bigger territorial problem than the German duke or prince who had escaped Machiavellian monism and had reformed his territory by the two sovereign powers of an invisible church and an efficient public service. The Presbyterians did not do justice to the size of this problem, and were doomed and replaced by Cromwell. The French democrats, aside from all their dreams of nature, were faced by the grim necessity of being a great power. They turned against their federalists quite brutally, because the latter were not equal to the magnitude of the task. The social revolutionaries in Russia made the same mistake, and were easily overthrown by the Bolsheviks, who immediately grasped the immense problem of organizing a continent instead of a nation.

This progressive ascent from little to big seems to form a natural climax. It is fascinating to see how each form of the rotation of government has been wrought out on an ascending scale. And this view frees the principle of rotation from its mechanical aspect of being merely a logical process. Though the four forms of government follow each other, they do not by any means repeat each other. Each revolution, standing on the shoulders of the foregoing, dares to go a step farther and attack a bigger problem in organization.

According to the pagan doctrine of mechanical change, one and the same community went from one temporal constitution to the next. In the Christian Era, coexistence brought with it the possibility of growth. The moral presence of the older revolution spurred on the younger sister each time. During the last four centuries, a consciousness of the forms already achieved has kept the young revolution from relapsing into chaos, and has sharpened her own duty to achieve more.

The rotation is not mechanical and not meaningless, because the starting point of the first revolution is preserved in the consciousness of all that follow. The four European divisions—Protestant prince, Puritan gentleman, Jacobin citizen, and Bolshevik proletarian—advance in a formation which in the army is called marching in echelon, each with its front clear of that ahead.

If the Marxian revolutionary theory were correct, the revolutions would arise successively in the same territory and in the same nation. Then the march in echelon would be impossible. The French gentry would have overthrown the French monarchy, French bourgeois the gentry, and French workers the bourgeoisie. The Lutheran princes all over Germany would have been beheaded by the "Junkers," the Junkers by the German middle classes, and the middle classes by the German Socialists. But that is completely chimerical. Luther's princes revolted for the whole German nation against the Italian pope. The English nation rebelled against the introduction of Continental monarchy into England, where it meant tyranny. The French nation expelled the megalomania which had been nourished by the *"gentilhomme"* ever since the British Glorious Revolution; and the Russians expelled European capitalism.

In this way each country could aim at the target of progress in its whole breadth and height. It did not move by simple reaction, what the Marxists call the dialectical process of thesis and antithesis. The pagan and mechanical philosophy of the Socialists made most of them overlook the simple facts and rules of coexistence. The English gentry, in overthrowing Lutheran monarchy, did not fall back into Catholicism. The Russians, in doing away with democracy, have not neglected the obligations imposed upon everybody by the French Revolution. The Russians must cling to national autonomy within their system, the British to Reformation, and the French to Parliament, though for a certain time the Presbyterians or Napoleon or Stalin miss the importance of this inevitable coherence and succession.

The whole question of progress depends on the possibility of coexistence of all the rungs of the ladder. In the woods, if you completely forget your starting point, you are likely to walk in a circle. To be driven in a vicious circle is the bogey and, in most cases, the real fate of pagan or primitive man. Their whole civilization is an endless repetition, without any opening or broadening out. Mr. Spengler, with his astounding primitivism, basks in this recurrence of spring, summer, autumn, and winter in each period of civilization. Primitive social groups, because they do not manage to coexist with their enemies, except by eating them, are bound to rotate in a vicious circle. The meaninglessness of so many South American revolutions, even as seen by the most sympathetic observers, such as Joseph Conrad in his *Nostromo*, is based on the fact that they follow each other in hopeless repetition. These revolutions are revolting to our human sensibilities because humanity yearns for growth and fulfilment. The great revolutions we have treated must be carefully distinguished from this mechanism of the vicious circle. They are great because they are sown in one common field of man's experience and hope. They all try to embrace all mankind; one after the other and one beside the other; like separate branches they are all grafted on the common tree of humanity.

This sequence in time and togetherness in space only became possible through a process of branching. The totalitarian faith of each revolution carries one country away from the centre, and to make up for this displacement the other countries, who either bear in themselves the seeds of an older revolution or hold back in expectation of their own day to come, rally all the more faithfully round the common centre.

Though the revolutions take their very name from the idea of rotation, of revolving, the wheel of a world revolution does more than turn in its old orbit. It moves forward along a new track and creates a new form of recurrent, repetitive life. Revolution in this sense does not shock us like the hundred revolutions in Mexico before Porfirio Diaz. Instead, it reproduces the institutions which breed and educate man. The Reformation or the Glorious Revolution produce their first results two hundred years after their outbreak, because it takes four or five generations to beget the perfect fruit of such a rebirth. Types like Pitt or Gladstone or Lincoln or Bach or Goethe had to be ripened by a long succession of unbroken faith, by the coherent labour of centuries.

Our revolutions must be raised to the square of their power before they can be understood in their deeper significance. They are not accidents of the kind which interest the reporter or the police, they are not sensational interruptions of an evolution which went on before and is resumed afterward. They change the face of the earth. Evolution is based on Revolution. It is sheer nonsense to put before us the choice between Evolution and Revolution. Revolution and Evolution are reciprocal ideas. Perhaps we do not like to believe this. But it is my disagreeable business, though myself a non-revolutionary, to deal with revolutions; it is not for the sake of originality that I attribute so much importance to revolution. No, creation goes on as God's creation has always done. A thunderstorm of destruction clears the air; then follows the low rustle of growth and reconstruction. We may assign the noise to the devil, and the still, small voice to God. But only wishful thinking can exclude either of these sounds.

The evolutionary theory of the nineteenth century has led us astray and taught us to use the words "evolution" and "revolution" as if they were mutually exclusive. Let the scientists re-examine their own concepts in the light of the real Darwin, who—as Mr. Brewster has made clear in his book on *Creation* —did not think of evolution in terms of an imperceptible gradation, but used it in the sense of creation. I prefer the word "creation" itself.

In history creation is going on all the time, and eternal recurrence of the created kinds is also going on all the time. The creative act that sets free new potentialities of mankind is properly called revolution. Not that creation is limited to revolutions; but in the course of history, the branches of the tree of mankind are truly regenerated—ay, by grafting they are really reproduced and changed, and this can only be done by a reconstruction of the great nurseries of men which we call nations.

Revolutions do not create man; they build nurseries, as we have said before, for his reproduction in a certain way and according to a certain type. There is no Christian country and no national character which can boast that it is founded on evolutionary institutions alone. "There is scarce a commonwealth in the world whose beginnings can in conscience be justified." (Hobbes.) Pope Pius II said that kingdoms were not taken by legality or righteousness but by conquest. The fact has been emphasized so often that these quotations could easily be multiplied—which only shows that the volcanic, illegal or pre-legal origin of all government has often been in the minds of thoughtful men.

The rise of a new sovereign is really the creation of a new kind of man, in a biological sense: how a monarchical Reformation remoulded the father of every family, how an aristocratic restoration reshaped every man, how national Revolution revolutionized every mind, and how a proletarian Revolution calls upon every body. Every father, every man, every mind, every body, are the respective consignees of the revolutionary freight. The revolutions address and extol different sides of man's being; but all the revolutions call upon him, conjure him up, usher him into the world with the same desperate faith in his responsibility. Every revolution we have investigated had something to say to every human being, not merely to a few. Monarchy, aristocracy, democracy and dictatorship cannot be distinguished by the more or less dependence they put in *every* member of the group. Every one of them uses the same passionate language to all. The Russian broadcasts in 1917 "to all" men are no more universal than the Lutheran pamphlets written for all Christians or the English Great Remonstrance addressed to the public.

"Open" Versus "Public"

The Revolutions occur as much in the open as any outbreak of war or fire or earthquake. Now "open" means more than "public." Open is as far above public as public stands above private. The lawyer knows private and public law; the politician or the newspaper man cannot afford to mistake private for public affairs. Private life and public life are separate worlds. But what of the open air, the immediate presence of earth and heaven, beyond the reach of social organization?

The openness of a revolution is the positive expression of its reality. Nothing is real which does not happen under God's open sky and under the evident pressure of our mother earth. The lawless character of Revolution may frighten us; its destruction of privacy and its contempt for public law make us tremble. But we ought not to deal with these greatest experiences of humanity in negative language. They are neither public nor private. We must find a positive word to explain their character. Whenever a name is found for a thing, whenever a thing is seized and held by a word, the world grows larger; when it is only described, men stay in their accustomed grooves.

All great revolutions re-create public law, public order, public spirit and public opinion; they all reform private customs, private manners and private feelings. They themselves must therefore live in a third dimension, beyond the reach of public law and private conviction. They live in the unprotected, unexplored and unorganized space which is hated by every civilization like hellfire itself—and which probably lies near hellfire. But it lies near heaven, too. Heaven and hell are the only words left to us for this character of openness and immediacy.

We nowadays have learned that hell and heaven are in our hearts. As the nineteenth century was private and individualistic, the heart, too, became a private business, and so the teaching of the gospel that heaven and hell are in our hearts reads to us like an inscription from a private album: it seems meant for private use alone.

But man's heart is the centre of creation. His is a world-heart. The son of man lives in the centre of the universe, he *is* the centre of the universe, and when his heart governs him he governs the world. Let us use an illustration for this way of life. Lovers have made a great fuss over the contrast between marriage in church and marriage by mutual private consent, yet there is little difference between them in actual fact. It is true, husband and wife can marry in public, with all the ceremonies and publicity of Church and State, or they can marry in private. But, whatever the forms, heaven and earth must participate in the wedding. The whole body must be rapt to its new calling, and the whole mind must be caught up into its new state of marriage. Then it is safe to say that something real has happened; when body and soul are completely dissolved and completely remade, you can be sure that this couple will become the founders of a new race, a new people, a new nation. After all, every marriage is the nucleus of a new race. It is nothing but statistical idolatry to judge a nation by its fifty or hundred millions of population. Those are mere abstractions. The people who marry change the nation unceasingly, if and when they meet in the presence of heaven and earth. Private relations or public ceremonies are *both* conventional disguises for the real story of marriage. The question is whether this young man and this young woman are going to be married under celestial ordination or by an "arbitrary power." Many a marriage, it is true, represents nothing but chance or a personal whim. The few that are something more regenerate their kind.

It is the same in politics. Some people rule, and more people vote, on arbitrary impulse. Those who do not, regenerate the standards of society. Revolutions try to regenerate the order of society by an inbreak of celestial powers. In both cases, hell is very near heaven. Whenever we venture to live in the open, we are exposed to all the risks of outdoor—i.e., of direct and immediate—life. Revolutions break into the framework of society from outside. They bear testimony to the very existence of free space around us. While we are under the law we are always anxious to forget its presence, like a good mother who thinks she can contract a marriage for her son. And because we are anxious to forget it, we are frightened by its sudden appearance. No power can derive its sovereignty from laws. Sovereignty comes first; everything else grows out of it. Luther first had to publish his Theses openly; the Roundheads first had to raise an army, and the Bastille first had to be destroyed before the new sovereign could become visible and begin to negotiate with the old powers.

This autocephalous origin of sovereignty is so certain that what we call the period of a revolution is nothing but the time it takes to make the new sovereign visible to the oldest veteran of the former world order. As soon as this oldest veteran has perceived its existence and its scope, peace can be restored and civil war can die down. But in this world of inertia it takes years, thirty or forty, before a new sovereign is recognized.

When Louis XVIII said on his return in 1815 that nothing had happened, only one more Frenchman was in France; the oldest veteran of monarchy had subscribed to the dogma of equality. When Charles V conceded the right of reformation to the territorial powers, and when the King of England acquiesced in a parliamentary church, the final word of a revolutionary period had been spoken. The same word which was high treason on the first day had at last become law, with the blessing of the very power against which it was first directed.

Every serious revolution begins, it seems, with a *"grande peur"* on the part of the population. *"Grande peur,"* great fear, was the name given to the inexplicable anxiety of the French nation in the summer of 1789. The same anxiety appeared in Germany in 1930. Three years before Hitler came into power the crisis could be felt and was felt by the im-

perilled educated classes in countless cases of nervous breakdown or temporary paralysis. For the Reformation, we know
that the whole German nation must have felt the meteoro-
logical signs. Two years before the bloodshed of the Peasants'
War, Luther, the successful, beloved, and admired Reformer,
wrote: "The signs of nature point certainly to a political revolution, and in especial by wars. Therefore I doubt not that
Germany faces either a terrible war or the Last Judgment."

This "*grande peur*" may be observed in the Middle Ages,
too, and I think for the sake of completeness, I may quote
Frederick II's exclamation in 1227:

"On us, then, the end of time has come, for not only in the
branches but in the roots as well the power of love is frozen. Not
only do peoples rise against peoples, and empires threaten empires,
not only do pestilence and hunger stir the hearts of the living with
terror, but the power of love itself, by which heaven and earth are
governed, seems now to be troubled, not in its later flowing, but
at the very *source*."

This great outcry leads us back to the connection between
the "Great Fear" and the drying-up of the power which governs heaven and earth. The great Revolutions break out whenever the power which has governed heaven and earth dries up
at the fountain-head. The great Revolutions seem to destroy
an existing order; but that is not true. They do not break out
until the old state of affairs is already ended, until the old
order of things has died and is no longer believed in by its
own beneficiaries. Ranke said of the Reformation: "When the
powers of the empire had grown suspicious of each other and
of themselves, the elementary forces on which the empire
rested began to stir. Lightnings flashed from the earth; the
currents of public life deserted their usual course; the storm
which had been heard rumbling so long in the depths rose
toward the upper regions; everything seemed ready for a complete overturn."

The ordinary laws of life, the fruit of millennia of struggle,
go to the devil when the spirit that animated them departs.
No positive law can hold a position which every good spirit

has deserted. When that happens, Goethe's words in *The Natural Daughter*[2] are in order:

> "This realm is threatened
> With utter ruin. For the elements
> That met to form its greatness will no longer
> Embrace each other with the force of love
> In unity unceasingly renewed.
> Now each evades the other, and withdraws
> Coldly into itself. Where is the might
> Of our forefathers' spirit, that once joined them,
> The warring elements, unto one end—
> The spirit which to this great people came
> As leader, as its own father and its king?
> Vanished forever! All that now remains
> Is a poor ghost that, striving against hope,
> Still dreams of winning back its lost possessions. . . ."

The state of Russia before the World War was described by Joseph de Maistre as that of a frozen corpse which would stink horribly in our nostrils when it thawed.

The power of love which governs heaven and earth is perishable indeed. Its stream sometimes runs dry. No "evolution" can guarantee mankind against this drying-up. We are no more protected against drought in politics than we are against drought in nature. But the "illimitable heart" by its illimitable Revolution restores the free working of the power which governs heaven and earth. When Dante wished to give the finishing touch to his pictures of the sins and virtues of mankind, he apostrophized the power which moves the sun and the other stars. He pointed to the equation between heaven and earth which we have rediscovered for modern times the, equation between human love and the rotations of the sky.

Heaven and earth are one. Christ has implanted love as the primary moving force in man. The times of Frederick II and Dante had the audacity to find one and the same principle at work in heaven and earth, in human and astral bodies. And today the physicists are finding one system of passionate

2 Act 5, Scene 8.

energies at work in the atom and in the universe. Niels Bohr describes the planetary system within the atom as one of successive catastrophes and readjustments, as in a Liliputian solar system.

Revolutions do nothing but readjust the equation between heart-power and social order. They come from the open and happen under the open sky. They bring about the Kingdom of God by force, and reach into the infinite in order to reform the finite.

Thus we have found out, for history and society, the important fact that open, public, and private are three different aggregate states for mankind. Unless it is *open*, no human law or personality is proof against the demons of life. No constitution can stand fast which has not sprung from war or revolution, which has not come from beyond public law or private pleasure. Political order is not meant for happiness or the full life or the greatest happiness of the greatest number. That is the cant of public-minded privateers who know nothing of the outdoor life of the pioneer, beyond good and evil, driven by the angels and demons of love and fear.

Revolutions come as a positive effort when the fear of a complete breakdown of order preys so terribly on the bowels of men that only a great courage and a great love can open the way to a new equilibrium of powers.

A Nation's Religion

The difference between politics and religion, confused as they are today, can be re-stated simply by the distinction of public and open. At no time can any group exist without religion and without public law. To reduce these two elements into one has often been tried, and never will succeed. Public Law asks the citizen for obedience, religion for worship. Any group obeys politically its legal ruler; but it worships religiously the opening of a new path out of chaos.

The gentry of England, the princes and professors of Germany, the *écrivains* of France and the Bolsheviks in Russia are, or were, revered by their respective nations as demigods. The worship bestowed on them as heroes corresponded to the peculiar religion these demigods stood for.

The witness of these supermen bridged the gulf between the natural man and the infinite by permitting him to take on a definite character. Much has been said and written about a nation's character. In most cases, I am sorry to say, the writers take the character like a stone, a piece of nature. This nation-alistic creed in fixed characters is charmingly defended by Mr. Madariaga, the long-time member of the League of Nations Council. In his *Englishmen, Frenchmen, Spaniards*, the under-lying principle is the eternity of a national character. The inevitable answer to this national fatalism is the "Revolt of the Masses," so ably described by Mr. Madariaga's fellow-countryman, Ortega y Gasset. How could it be otherwise? A man who believes in fixed types should not groan when living men do not respond. I know that the average psychologist thinks he is delving very, very deep when he says that French-men are democratic, Germans obedient, and that the English have a natural liking for aristocrats. But is this not poor psy-chology? Is it not intolerable for any human being to feel himself condemned once for all, by the mere accident of birth, to a fixed character? In the field of political or moral values we are all competitors, all of divine nature, all changeable and transformable. But we are "nationals" because we are men, capable of feeling gratitude and of responding to this feel-ing. Thinking and thanking belong together. As long as we have reason to be grateful we shall always respect and repeat the reasoning of our elders. A nation never forgets its interval in the open, between fear and faith, hate and love; for in it this certain section of humanity came into contact with God. If anyone paves a road into a new love, a new faith, a new governing power, he becomes the legislator of the revolution. He vanquishes the fear of hell and disintegration: "They have knocked at all the doors that led nowhere, and the only one by which they can enter, and for which they searched centuries long, opens suddenly." (Proust.) Since he seals this new cove-nant between the Creator and his frightened and fearing creatures, he establishes a new faith and a new order of things. Since this order is not based on reason but on deliverance from fear, it very often takes a long time to make the new way practicable for every-day work. However, the abolition of fear precedes all practical action. For the creator of a new heaven and a new earth transforms the people. And in return his own kind becomes a severed caste and governing class; his social function becomes a church-like institution for his country.

The prince, the gentleman, the scholar, the minister—they have taught the Germans and the English when they were despondent how to pray so that they might be heard. The formula of this prayer becomes the secret law of the land, the very core of the nation's language, and makes the use of any foreign political vocabulary impossible. It produces a kind of immunity.

The German language in 1649 or 1688 was so full of "Reformation," of chorales and the Lutheran Bible, that when a historian tried to find the reaction of German public opinion to Cromwell and William III he was overcome by disappointment. To no revolution did Germany react so little as to the English. Even today, in the vocabulary of German political language the political concepts of England stand like foreign bodies, unconnected with the native tradition, whereas "cavalier" and "feudal" are high praise in a German mouth. This is because the British Revolution came too early to find a door open. The love of the Reformation had not yet died down. The Fronde in France was much more dangerous in its imitation of the Puritans.

Today, the same French nation cannot swallow the Russian Revolution: they are simply too near their own great revolutionary past. Nobody can think of Poincaré and Stalin, Clemenceau and Lenin, as contemporaries. They live on different planets, as far apart as Venus and Neptune. And this is certainly no quibble, but a serious attempt to explain the depth and stability of our political religion or our religious politics.

No man is a European who has not been educated by certain church-like institutions in his own country, institutions created once and forever by a revolution which teaches him faith, hope, and love, but mainly love. The languages of Europe are not materialistic facts, but creative expressions of a certain side of the Christian faith, used by a certain political class in a certain section of the continent.

The successful creation of a new political language by a new class, in a new section of the continent, is called a Revolution; and the territory within which it succeeds and the people whom it transforms are the components of a nation. Nations are the products of Revolutions.

Each nation depends upon a leading class, which from its inspired stand in the open danger and open warfare of revolution becomes the governing class in public law and the model of private life. The Bolshevik party in Russia, the religious party in Germany, the parliamentary party in England, the civic party in France, are not fractions of an existing nation, but the *raison d'être* of the whole.

European Dictionary

In accordance with this rule, no country's political grammar can be literally translated into that of any other. A group of institutes from America and various European countries recently compiled a dictionary of political science. The method it followed was simply to ask each national group to contribute an article on each subject: Italians, French, Germans, and English were to work out a series on State, Government, Nation, Parliament, etc. Each group worked and kneaded those poor words in its own fashion, according to the predilection or the indifference of its own nation toward each one.

But these political words are more than scholars' terms; they lie at the heart of a nation's becoming and making. There is no reciprocity between "nation" in English and "nation" in French, nor between "civilization" in Italian and in German. A system of European political language can never be based on the meretricious superstition that these words can go through an international clearing-house. They are the minted gold of a nation's treasure. Let us give some examples:

GERMAN	ENGLISH	FRENCH	RUSSIAN
Cultivated	Countrified	Civilized	Electrified
Staat	Commonwealth	Nation	Soviets
Every Christian	Every man	Every individual	Every body
Magistrates	Commons	Intellectuals	Communists
Katheder	Pulpit	Tribune	
Prince	Gentleman	Citizen	Proletarian
High	Old	New	Functioning
Hochgesinnt	Public-spirited	Grand	
General principle	Public spirit	Esprit	
Hochwohlgeboren		Élite	Quality
		Intellectuelle	
Gemeine Mann	The poor	Les Illettrés	Quantity
Protestant	Whig	Liberal	
Magister, Dr.	Minister	Écrivain	
Billigkeit	Common sense	Bon sens	
(= Equity)			
Pflicht (= Duty)	Right	Idée	Function
Geheimrat	M.P.	Académicien	
Sehr geehrter	Dear Sir	Cher ami	Tovarich
Herr	William		(comrade)
Gewissenhaft	Righteous	Bon	Efficient
(conscientious)			
Beamter ("Rat")	J.P.	Légion d'Honneur	
Geist	World	Nature	Society

The vocabulary of High in German and of Low in English has created a network of derivations. *Hoheit, Hochwohlgeboren, leutselig, herablassend, Hochachtungsvoll, Hochgemut, Hochgeehrt*, should be set off against Low, Low Church, Lower House, common sense, minister, ministry. Or the German group around *Mut* (*Übermut, Grossmut, Demut, Armut*, ect.) against the English "quiet," "calm," "discreet," "demure," "reserved," etc., etc.

The positive sense of *"Hochschule"* in German contrasts with the negative sense of high-brow, high church in England. A German boy is recommended as "highly" gifted; in England he does better if he has "common sense." And the French language has still a third creed. The French, being above all individuals, translate "common" by "good." All the English compounds of "well" or "good" are of French origin. In 1789 there was published in Paris the little *Code of Human Reason*, by Barbeu du Bourg, which says, "Man needs at least three things for his happiness: Health, common sense, and a clear conscience, and man needs nothing but three things: Health, common sense, and a clear conscience." But in French it runs "le *bon*heur requires *bonne* santé, *bon* sens, *bonne* conscience." The Frenchman has *bon sens* and a *bonne conscience*. But good sense and common sense are very different. Luther would never have permitted himself to call anything in his own sinful self good. Luther's conscience was *pure*, genuine; a gentleman's motives had to be based on the common weal.

Some words have invaded the European world without keeping their national stamp because whenever an institution was derived from one particular country the rest of Europe took over the terms and names for its functioning in a mechanical and superficial way. "Republic," "revolutionary" and "national" are French; "supremacy," "sovereignty," and "Ph.D." are German; "parliament," "country" and "local government" are English.

The dictionary will tell you that most of these words are Latin. "Sovereign" was invented by a French thinker. "Supremacy" occurs in Henry VIII's "Act of Supremacy." Why, then, are they German? And are not "Country" (*comitatus*) and "republic" simply international? Parliament is a French word translated from the good old German "sprakka," i.e., *colloquium*; but the Germans despised parliaments, the English believed in them.

Any number of such misunderstandings could be cited. Our list on the word "nation" is a most confusing example. This word, which our statesmen are fond of pulling like an organ-stop, sounds a different note in every country. Diplomats should be required to say, when they use it, whether they are speaking French or Russian or English or German.

Each of these European languages can be heard anywhere in Europe: they are exchanged freely among the different countries. There are Catholics in Germany, Tories in England, royalists in France, and the "*spez*" in Russia, to speak the pre-revolutionary language. To give one good example, the Royalists in France went so far as to preserve for a century the old Versailles pronunciation of the word King, calling him not "Roa," like the Parisians, but Roy, like the English "royal," as in the days when the language of Versailles was the standard.

The later revolutionary languages also invade the precincts of the older European stocks. Thought jumps lightly over all frontiers. Communists are everywhere, Fascist "shirts" are everywhere. The same was of course true of the Jacobins in 1800, who could be found everywhere, and of the Conservatives after 1815, who reacted as the Fascists are doing today. For the sake of decency the Jacobins turned "Liberal," and as Liberals they conquered a world which had been closed to them as long as they were called Jacobins. The pietistic affiliates which the Whigs, the gentry, and their ministers had on the Continent were no stronger than the friends the Lutherans had in England in the seventeenth century. At that time Lutheranism was so much of a uniting force that even Henry VIII thought of joining its League. "It is not improbable that the fate of Henry VIII's second wife, Anne Boleyn, was sealed by Henry's failure to gain for his second marriage the endorsement of the Wittenberg faculty."

Is it not strange that within a year or two, any national upheaval born of truly revolutionary ambition can find supporters in every country?

It is a fact, though an incredible one to the superficial democrat, that Mr. Everyman is by no means necessarily on the side of democracy in these processes of political infection. Dictators or monarchs have supporters quite as ready and quite as devout, when the time is ripe. "Democracy" has no surer approach to the masses of men than the other three forms of government. Each form seems, strangely enough, to express a popular longing. The German civil law, the English Common Law, the French laws of nature, the Russian laws of Lenin, were all welcomed with fierce enthusiasm.

The forms of government are more than the superficial garb of certain office-holders. At least for the Europe of modern times, they are the flesh and blood of a particular body politic.

The country which produces the new form is given to it heart and soul. It must let some adherents of the pre-revolutionary order survive, it is true (Catholics, Nobles, Aristocrats, Bourgeois); but on the whole its creative effort absorbs all the religious energies of the nation. This process reaches the population of the whole country. Everybody is conscience-stricken, for everybody shared in the *"grande peur,"* and by that shock was prepared for a break-up of his inner being. Monarchy or aristocracy or democracy are poor terms to define the power which so deeply ploughs the clods of a nation and kneads the clay of man into a new image of God.

Bionomics of Western Man

This totalitarian character of the Revolutions we have studied obliges us to insert them as stages in the natural creation of mankind. Such Revolutions carry on the process of creation. Thus political history ceases to be outside nature: man and the other forms of creation are closely akin, with the great difference that man was not created a hundred thousand years ago, but is being made before our eyes.

Men are reproduced, regenerated and physically influenced by the great Revolutions we have already observed. The European nations did not exist in 1000. Most of them were shaped in 1500. Today they are well-known to all of us, some of them already in decay, or reorganization, but certainly all of them transient. What existed before they were born? Or shall we say that the Revolutions did not really create them, but only built a kind of well-kerb around each nation's most particular qualities so that they might flow and come forth forever?

In each case, it was the revolutionary setting of the nation which enabled it to make its contribution to the world at large. Civil government, parliamentarism, democracy, planning, are developed in one country as an ultimate end, whereas all the others can use it as a thing of relative importance. When parents, for example, compare Russia and her terrible sufferings with France or America, they thank God that they need not bring up their children in Russia. The Roosevelt New Deal is less painful than the *Piatiletka*. The novelties of the French Revolution were introduced into England or Germany with less murder and warfare than France had to undergo. But we can be sure that without the French Revolution, England would not have seen the Reform Bill of 1832 nor Germany its Revolution of 1848. The New Deal and the devaluation of the dollar are unthinkable without a preceding Bolshevik Revolution. The Great Revolutions are eccentric, they exaggerate, they are brutal and cruel. But the life of the rest of the world is regenerated by their outbreak. It may seem doubtful who gains more, the revolutionized country or its partners. One thing is certain, the old forms of civilization, stagnating, their circulation clotted, are regenerated by the power of the new form. Life is regenerated in the rest of the world whenever a new form joins the older ones.

Not that the older forms become superfluous. A partisan of fascism thinks, of course, that democracy is doomed, as the liberals bet in 1830 that the House of Lords in England would disappear within ten years. But the House of Lords exists, kings govern, and French democracy will exist in 1940 or 1950. Perhaps the addition of a new form even relieves and eases the older forms of a part of their burden. They recover. Monarchy in Germany experienced a regeneration after the Napoleonic wars, and the regeneration of the English system after 1815 is well-known.

The biological secret of eternal life can, perhaps, be formulated thus: Lest the old kinds die or stagnate, a new kind branches off from the tree of life. By reason of this flowing forth of life into new forms the forms already existing are able to survive. The revolutionary creation of one new kind permits the evolution of the older kinds.

CHAPTER 12

IMMIGRATION OF THE SPIRIT

An Interview on Radio Bremen[1]

ANOTHER SCHOLAR WHO CAME back to Germany as a visiting professor at the University of Münster was Eugen Rosenstock-Huessy. When we made contact with him and outlined the major questions to be considered, he pointed out that the consequences of immigration, rather than those of emigration undoubtedly should be more heavily emphasized. He therefore considered our questions from this perspective.

Question: Professor Rosenstock-Huessy, you were a visiting professor at the University of Münster in 1958 and lectured one semester for German students. Was this your first visit since emigrating?

Answer: No. I left in 1933; in 1950 I was invited by my old law and political science colleagues in Göttingen to lecture on the history of German law or on another topic I might prefer. While selecting the topic for my lectures I deliberated unhurriedly over the subject matter I now treat in America. I entered into fresh territory when I left Germany, for my old specialty was inaccessible for Americans. By steps, in 1950, '52, '56, '57, '58, I learned to teach here in Germany the subject I had mastered in America. Thus, I laid down back here on German soil a roadway leading into the new field of learning founded in America. It was very arduous. It certainly is most difficult to appear at a former home in new clothes and to make manifest what one has attained in such a way that the expert knowledge

[1] Translated from *"Auszug des Geistes,"* ("Exodus of The Spirt)" Radio Bremen, *Bremer Beiträge IV,* Verlag B. C. Heye & Co., Bremen, 1962, pp. 106–126.

people expect is overshadowed by what one has learned in addition.

All immigrants probably have difficulties in their relationship to the old world which focuses attention only on the moment of departure and says, "When he returns he'll be just the same." That's true only to a limited extent. Among the most important things I have learned in America is this: much of the German or European fund of knowledge is not suited for Americans. It is a great pity that the Americans in their humility, modesty, and intellectual unpretentiousness have had European cultural wares transmitted to them by specialists who continued to think in European categories. I was the first professor in my college who spelled out the American contributions to philosophy in a special course. In my other teaching specialties as well I took care not to simply continue speaking as I had in Germany, but rather to base my teaching on the entirely different conceptions of my students over there in the new world.

The world in which the American student who comes to me at about twenty years of age really has confidence is the world of sport. This world encompasses all of his virtues and experiences, affections and interests; therefore I have built my entire sociology around the experiences an American has in athletics and games. Through this approach I have found confirmed what stood in my earlier German sociology, stimulating no interest at all in Europe: people preserve their thousand-year-old experiences in the world of play. The law court proceedings of the old Germans still haunt the game of forfeits: "What should he do, whose forfeit have I in my hand?"

War, contracting a marriage, and every other significant act is similarly contained in some form of game. It is just played with. In Europe one may build a sociology on art, in America on sport. The experiences of the Europeans with Bach, Wagner, and Beethoven must be transposed so-to-say to athletic experiences. In America you can't make reference to the experiences a young man has with the fine arts, as you can in Italy. You can, however, very probably remind him that he learned to live lyrically while skiing, dramatically in football, epically through swimming, so that he suddenly recognizes that these events he lived through unconsciously in a group represent his first philosophy. In short, he already knows quite a lot about life. If I had mixed in some sort of European esthetics, sociology, or romantics, my students would have had the feeling I was trying to plant a European head on their American heart. I guarded against that scrupulously.

Question: When you say that today, you're speaking from experience. But in 1933 when you made the decision to leave Germany and Europe, you certainly didn't know what to expect. Would you think back once again to this time and perhaps tell us what you left behind in order to go forth, and how you attempted to master all the new things you encountered?

Answer: That is a very serious question. My answer may sound somewhat immodest, but I'll tell the truth. When the war came to an end in 1918 I saw not only that the war was lost, but that Europe's position of supremacy in the world was also a thing of the past. Germany had lost its claim to sovereign national power, and this claim might be asserted in the future only through the permission of the whole world. I foresaw Hitler's advent and published and said as early as 1919 that we must attempt to survive him; after Hitler we would be forced for the first time to recognize the real results of the world war. In 1919 I really didn't think I had the right to leave conquered Germany. I had to stay at the wake, so-to-speak, and thought, since I loved the country dearly and had been its soldier and teacher, I had to hold out as long as possible and prepare for the future. I founded the work-service, I established labor newspapers, I abstained from exercising or hid my academic prerogatives as much as possible and tried to live with men who would have to live in the future without romantic, ideal, and patriotic models. I tried to make them capable and strong for life.

No handsomer compliment could have been given me on my seventieth birthday than that spoken by Walter Hammer, calling me the patriarch of the Kreisau Kreis.[2] For many of the men of the Kreisau Kreis had been in the work-service camps we developed in the nineteen twenties in Germany. But when nothing helped, and when all I had predicted broke forth in

---

[2] A group of Germans who conspired against Hitler.

1933, I didn't hesitate long. I was convinced I was no longer required to stay indefinitely through the impossible. I went to the new world, not with some sort of plans or intentions, but with the feeling all those drawn toward America to become Americans share, and in the faith attributed to Abraham in the Bible. He too had known nothing more than that he should go out from the land of his fathers. He had no suspicion of what awaited him. I can assure you, it's the same when one lands in New York. One really doesn't know what's going to happen. One doesn't hope, but does have faith.

I took along from the old world into the new a readiness to give up my previous activities. For instance I immediately resigned the chairmanship of the World League for Adult Education in London, which I certainly didn't have to do. It was after all an international organization. I was probably very foolish to give up the only position I had in the whole world. I was elected in 1929 to this office *ad personam* by 400 delegates from throughout the world, from Australia to Timbuktu. After all, I was a professor in Germany, a respected man; but it would have been a breach of confidence for me to continue to serve in this office as a mere emigrant. By the resignation of this office you can see how radically I made the separation from my previous world.

If you would like to extract a possible moral for emigrants headed for America from this resignation, I'll try to help you. You see, at 45 I was already an established man, a clearly defined profile. I was listed not only in Kürschner[3] but also in the *Konversationslexikon*. It was completely clear to me that America would simply not be able to admit such a fully developed character as an immigrant. America only had to extend me an opportunity to make a new beginning and then to see what I, with my particular gifts, might be capable of. I was ready to become a farmer or businessman or to remain a professor or to become a professor of something else. Everything remained to be seen. So in the first years, about seven, until the outbreak of the second world war, I let myself be carried

[3] *Kürschners Deutschen Gelehrtenkalender*, a reference book or "who's who" of German scholars.

by the waves. I was knocked about quite a bit, then finally had the good fortune not to be stranded in the attic of the academic world, but rather to get solid ground under my feet. I am now living in the country. It is no accident, but a great blessing, for it has given me enough endurance and patience to be content without my official position in Europe.

Question: Was anyone able to help you in the first years? After all, you still had to live. You arrived in New York and, as you said, when an individual stands in that city he is faced with the question—what now?

Answer: I knew only one thing about America: New York is not part of America. I quipped at the time, "I want to go to America, but not to New York!" So I traveled further on the evening of my arrival, at least as far as Boston. From Boston I was pulled to New Hampshire and from New Hampshire to Vermont, deeper and deeper into the experience of the small community, independent of Europe. I learned that in America the power to conduct political affairs properly is formed and maintained in small groups, not in the big cities which so fascinate the foreigner. I would recommend to all my friends coming to America to go first of all to a town in Pennsylvania or New England before seeing a major city. For even though the Americans have built these big cities from the villages and towns, the cities are still not America, not even today.

Well, that's too far afield. I found, of course, infinitely great willingness to help, for example through an invitation to give a course at Harvard University without pay. I had to defray all expenses with my own means like a *Privatdozent.* I found friends through these lectures; some were very surprised that they found themselves involved at all with a man from Germany. A great Francophile told me in 1933, "You're the first German I've listened to since the world war." This very man contributed toward our future in America and helped us as only an American can. Just after the outbreak of the war for America in Pearl Harbor he sent to us in the country, quite out of the blue, the last washing machine he was still able to purchase in Boston. It came with the brief note: "During the war it will be hard for you to survive in your solitude. You won't find help. Here is at least a machine that will make life easier for you and your wife." This was the man who, prior to 1933, hadn't spoken to a German.

Such stories must be told more often, but it must be added that the great "welcome-club" called America was still in business in 1933. Today, however, after the disillusionment it experienced through two world wars in Europe, it no longer reacts in the same way. Europe correlates American dates, the history of its soul, too naively with European history. When I landed in America in 1933, a European with so much education and learning was still as much of an object for exhibit as say in 1890. Even the First World War hadn't altered the readiness of Americans to let themselves be taught by Europeans. Now things are different.

Question: You just said you had been invited to teach at Harvard University, but weren't paid. What did they expect from you? Why were you given the chance and what did you live on?

Answer: That too is an amusing story. I had earned a reputation in Europe through work-camps for laborers, farmers, and students. They spread like wildfire from the original camp we established in Silesia throughout central Europe. An American professor at Harvard had learned of this through my dearest student who had co-founded these camps and was then studying at Harvard. This was something new and original, and he had one of his students write a small brochure on the camps as an example for America too. The student and the professor both came to Germany. I also invited this professor to give a lecture at the University of Breslau, and we became friends. Now since he had been in my house and had seen what I did and taught, and I had shown him hospitality, I could write to him on February 1, 1933: "My dear Sir, Germany has just spit out 400 years of higher education and statehood. I want to leave. Can you help me?" He wrote back, "I can extend an invitation to you, but it is too late to secure any sort of support."

Then I went to the ministry of culture in Berlin. This too may be worth some reflection historically. I found that the new possessors of power felt very unsure of themselves. They did not yet have the security that seemed to distinguish them in later years. I don't know that they felt so secure. But in February 1933 they were as yet in a precarious position. I came before them and said: "You can destroy me or you can help me to start a new life over there. What's your decision?" To which the official said, "We'd prefer to help you build a new existence. I will transfer at least a small part of your salary to you in America." And that he honestly did for a year. It was little enough, only 150 dollars a month. Anyone who has been in America knows one can't live well on that, but it was possible to get by. Until 1941, until Pearl Harbor, I was on leave of absence each year. I emigrated, then, not at all like the poor people suddenly placed by a swift kick face to face with destitution. On the contrary, I retained throughout this whole eight or nine year period a comforting feeling from having made up my mind and made a decision concerning Hitler spontaneously, not under duress. I believe that was very good for my soul.

You'll be interested too in the fact that I returned to Europe once more in 1935. This is an unrecognized rule. I also had my son travel back to Europe again in 1937. Both of us then returned to our new homeland with great enthusiasm. Many who left missed this first visit back in the old European homeland, and this reconfirmation that one must henceforth pitch one's tent in America. They first landed in America at the last moment, in 1938 after the first pogrom, or even in 1939. They had to cling to the United States already torn by war; they were never really at home. They harbored a glowing desire for Europe in their hearts and then, in 1947 or 1948, they hurried back to a Europe which had been smashed to bits. This return then was mostly a very painful experience on both sides. Either they remained in Europe and set the American experience aside as radically as possible, or they remained disillusioned. I was spared that. During my visit in Europe in 1935 I travelled to Germany, met many friends, and that gave my farewell its finality. I would like to say I discovered a law of emigration: a man emigrates the first time with his head, will, and thoughts, and has to throw his feelings and irrational person over the hurdle in a second attempt. Well, it all worked out very nicely just because I did not complain in 1933 about having to leave. Because I saw this misfortune coming so far in advance, I just said—that's it.

Question: After the lectures as a visitor, did you secure a teaching post at Harvard?

Answer: It's very noteworthy that you want to know the details. Since Harvard University was a very learned institution, it got around very quickly that I lectured on the European revolutions with great success and had a great following. The best men at Harvard, even President Conant, who later became known in Bonn as the American ambassador, took great pains to keep me there. First they gave me the Kuno-Francke Professorship for German Art and Culture. At that time this chair provided a one-year appointment for a visiting professor; each year it was to be given to another. So, surprisingly enough, I represented Germany in America, for that was my office as professor for German Art and Culture. I was transferred later to the History and Philosophy Department and did to complete satisfaction, I believe, all that could be required of one whose mother tongue was not English. But I had no difficulties: I had spoken English ever since my youth.

But then there cropped up at Harvard the same conflict I had had to fight through in Europe in agnostic modern colleges. I can't complain about this either. At Harvard they were just tuned in for doctrinaire positivists. That I spoke completely forthrightly in my lectures on the destiny of mankind and the history of salvation and the Lord God hurt me, since I didn't fit into the communist groove. The American intelligentsia in 1933 was interested in nothing but Russia. Today it is difficult to imagine to what an extent the youth of America held as unmodern a man who didn't profess himself to be a communist. I'm revealing no secret. I've said and published often that even the great old English philosopher Alfred Whitehead, who wanted to help me, gave me a private lecture in his house in which he said, "My dear friend, we all want to help you, but it would be so much easier if you were a communist. Then all these atheists who despair over you now because you trouble about religion would help you. Christianity is, after all, obsolete.

I can't become a communist any more," he said—he was seventy years old at the time—"but you still could be one." Well, as you can imagine, I didn't abandon my conviction so simply. He understood that.

Anyway, it came to a crash. A group of energetic young men went to President Conant and told him the reputation of Harvard would be disfigured if a believing man were to lecture on history, sociology, law, speech, and more besides. Then I was very delicately shoved into the department of theology, the so-called Divinity School, because they didn't wish me ill, but considered me an impossible thinker. That, of course, amounted to a first-class burial. I didn't want to be a theologian. I was and am no theologian. I was then helped as one who seems unsuited for Harvard is helped; I was referred to Dartmouth College in New Hampshire. People there were very happy to have a man who offered new courses. I was given a free hand and was able to fulfill my ideals, to speak on American themes for Americans. I lectured on American philosophy, taught about the family and sport, emigration and colonization and the accomplishments of the pioneers.

I founded Camp William James, a camp in the sense of William James, the greatest American thinker. He had already sensed in 1910 that the time of great wars must come to an end if mankind didn't want self destruction, and demanded that the warlike traits, the heroism in the life of each and every young man must be granted as his right without bloodshed and murder. Since I had already aspired toward similar goals in Europe, it was not difficult for me to insipre young men to found a work service with such a purpose in America too. Accordingly I moved to the country, for we directed our work toward the reconstruction of the declining state of Vermont. I've remained there, keeping a foot in the earth of the country. In the small community, in which I now live, I was accepted extremely slowly. It's been a long road. I believe that now, after 23 years, I'm one of the senior residents in the village. We have considerable moving and relocation. It's no exaggeration: now I belong more to the older inhabitants than to the newcomers. Well, one can't decide such things for oneself. At any rate, I've reserved my cemetery plot in the oldest cemetery of the oldest settlement of the village.

Question: If you feel at home in your village today, it has been achieved through years of effort. If you with your intelligence had to take leave from what you once were, and are satisfied with what you are and have today, and have built an intellectual world you can call your own, then a thousand thoughts must have been rearranged in the process. You've attained another view of Europe from America, and probably have conserved and lived in other ways your European traits. And therefore, I think we still have to speak of the difficulties.

Answer: All right, I'll try, as far as that is possible and to the extent to which a European can have any conception at all of the position a teacher had in America. The teaching function in America, until recent years, had been women's work. All teaching up to higher education, therefore, had a completely different appearance than in Germany or even in France. The aggressive manly, forward-driving, innovative, revolutionary element in the whole art of teaching in the United States was lacking. Teaching was a quieting sort of ornament by which youth learned to associate with the beautiful, agreeable, and even true things of life of the great past. But it was all based on thinking back, not on thinking forward.

Europeans, hard pressed as they were by limited space, threatened by wars, envied by neighbors, have searched for the future in thought. The Promethean element, the ability to think in advance, has driven European science from one new feat to the next. Europeans have driven science in America forward, and we still don't know whether a tradition of genuine research can be built from many generations of Americans alone. I have my doubts on account of the excess of money available for "research." Money corrupts. If I have to solicit great foundations for money for my research, then I have to propose something which is already obsolete for me. I know no researcher who in the first moment of a new inspiration could have found the sympathy and approval of the establishment. Whether it's Galileo, Copernicus, Fichte, or I myself, it's always the same: the new thought has to break through in battle against the vested interests, the power of the establishment, the conception of squandered money, against money itself—in short, against powers of all sorts.

Of course, when one has access to 200 million dollars a year for research, the great danger arises that the foolish, the pedestrian, the biased research, that which just goes along in the tracks others have laid, will be unfairly privileged at the expense of research that goes boldly forth on a brand new tack. Perhaps the Americans in brilliant carelessness may find ways to support dauntlessly the new as well as the trivial. Would you like to hear an example? In the first year of the Ford Foundation Paul Hoffmann, who then served as its president, had the brilliance and courage to say, "I'll support only projects that are already under way." He wanted to support the bold spirits who wanted to and were able to carry their own ideas ahead in the face of danger, want, indebtedness. The whole apparatus of his foundation, however, contradicted such a search for unknown talents. They just made up their own program and developed their own philosophy, as it's so fondly called in America.

I've seen terrible instances where young people have asked themselves, "What do I have to propose to get money?" A man who does that once in his life has ceased to be of any possible significance for science. He is corrupt. This great danger for the future of science in America distresses and oppresses me. It doesn't rest on anyone's evil will, but on the opposite; it is caused by too much good will, by the belief that spirit can be aroused by cash. Of course that's impossible.

I haven't been personally involved in all these things. I'm just telling of how difficult it is in America to really stick to and go further along the intellectual paths Europeans try to continue over there.

Each generation in America has been kept spiritually and intellectually alive either through visiting Europe or through importing Europeans. It's not clear how things may continue if the importation of European intelligence is now cut off, if the Americans say to one another in a completely understandable reaction, "We've brought over too many of these European intellectuals. We can assimilate the poor Iranians, the Poles, even the Chinese and Japanese in California to a certain extent; but we can accept European scholars and artists only in very limited numbers." From 1933 until today we've provided something for the Americans—I'd like to mention again, I definitely consider myself one—something they haven't grasped. We've wanted to instruct them too with our judgments, theories, teaching, and taste. I consider myself a member of the last generation of emigrants in America who began with a clean slate and unfortunately, and applies to me too, exist too largely through the printed word.

America is in a critical situation today. The obvious objective intellectual supplies from Europe may be choked off before organs for a continual reproduction of the intellectual and spiritual life, a constant renewal, a free research, an aggressively manly, forward-striding, revolutionary upbringing of youth are developed.

Question: Have you had significant contact with other emigrants?

Answer: The greater the success of the emigrant, the more he has to attempt to cease being a European. You can ask all my fellow emigrants. The success of the emigrant depends directly on whether he manages to avoid becoming identified with all the others and instead is lucky and becomes more than just one of many, which is not so simple in America. How is one supposed to master his own destiny, become a person, experience what unique things can be achieved in this land as a member of a great group of foreign professors which has to be digested? This is probably the most marvelous thing about the emigration: through it one sheds various roles like snakeskins until finally one reaches a definite final hide. At my age one can no longer become an American, not in the sense of a native-born American. I have no illusions about that. Nor has that ever been my ambition.

But I have used up so much courage going through these changes. I shouldn't neglect entirely the comic aspects of these metamorphoses. When the war broke forth in 1941 I who had emigrated with the coming of National Socialism was con-

sidered in my village as an obvious agent of Hitler. These good
New Englanders had no other Germans they might have reacted against. The pastor of my church congregation, being of
German origins three generations back, told me quite simply I
would undoubtedly understand that he couldn't speak with me
during the war. Others pleasantly told me I had better not let
myself be seen on the main street of the village for the next few
years. Still other friends met in my home and deliberated on
how they might drum me out. Then they published a very beautiful testimonial about me in the newspaper. They dug up old
documents from my time at Harvard and found among them a
protest statement from the student body at Breslau—naturally
of a purely Nazi stripe—in which they protested against my
betrayal of German culture at Harvard as Kuno-Francke professor. Well, that was proof for my neighbors that I was a respectable man, and with the help of this testimonial I remained un-
disturbed at Dartmouth College.

The second round had another visage. In 1947–1949 the
great anti-communist McCarthy investigations began. Before
this officially started, my son who was in government service as
a doctor was attacked by a colleague who envied his career and
accused him of being under the determining influence of a
leading communist. This communist was supposed to be I. We
had to go to Washington, there was a big trial, and I had to
prove I was no communist. It's rather comical to be fought one
time as a National Socialist spy and another time as a communist. To complete the farce or demonic tale: in 1934 a very
famous emigrant—I won't name him, he's very renowned—
traveled to Harvard and said, "Eugen, you must assure me con-
vincingly that you're not a Nazi spy." I just laughed. We've
remained good friends to the present, and he has probably long
forgotten this incident.

But such mutually and totally incompatible situations do
occur in the course of 25 years, and I was already accustomed
to such afflictions in Europe. Consequently, I didn't consider
these happenings in America tragic. Of course, when I was sus-
pected of being a leading communist I really didn't know what
to do. It's not so easy for one to prove one is not a communist,

since communists lie and disguise themselves, and therefore in the end even the Christian religious writings I had perpetrated might be dismissed as mere camouflage. Such situations in America are resolved through the courage of individuals. Completely unexceptional people suddenly step forward and support an accused man. The witnesses I was able to bring with me to Washington gave me the greatest feeling of happiness. In America new friendships and groups one could not at all have counted upon form and prove their worth again and again. And what came to pass then—in 1948 I think, but I'm not sure of the year—ended in the triumph of friendship and the willingness of good neighbors to help.

Question: May I come back once more to 1950, Professor Rosenstock-Huessy, to the time when you received your first invitation to return to Germany? What did you find in Germany? How did you react to Germany?

Answer: I was very lucky there, too. When I look back now from 1958, I was perhaps the slowest of those who returned. I was one of the first to leave and one of the last to come back. I returned in 1950 with a divided heart, because I knew I was being called back to an old cliché, to an office I had long since cast off within that of an historian of German law. I accepted because I was very indebted to my friend Hans Thieme who invited me. He knew of my struggles in Breslau because he had served there as a young instructor, and I knew he wanted me to come. But in the course of the semester I first had to convince the university as a whole that I was not just an unconditional returner, but rather I had led a new life filled with new content.

Fortunately, the matter didn't end there. I had friends in Germany outside the university who had continued my work of the nineteen twenties. First of all my friend Georg Müller revealed Bethel[4] near Bielefeld to me. Bethel's founder, Bodelschwingh, demanded that Bethel stand firmer than the state of Prussia. And it did; I returned in 1950 to a Germany represented by Bethel which had had the power to survive even the destruction of Prussia. May I say that ever since, in these eight years, it

[4] A great institution of the Protestant Church, caring for the sick and disabled, Bethel is a community of its own.

was a privilege to meet with circles of men and women who had been capable of surviving the political confusions through the strength of a higher sphere. It caused me to rejoice. A bent towards the powers that strengthen men in Europe as in America, completely independently of national character, was involved. Finally, I was even given an honorary degree, as doctor of theology. I have been really favored, for I can't ascribe to myself anything meriting this friendship I found in Europe.

In 1952 I was called to Germany by Bavarian public educators. They were kind enough to remember my actions between 1918 and 1933 in the area of public education and wanted me to instruct a new staff of educators. This I did. About 400 men and women came through these weeks of schooling which we lived together within small living communities. I'm glad I didn't miss that. The weeks in the poison gas shell storehouse in Traunreudt, that today has been transformed by Siemens into a factory, in particular belong with the finest experiences of my life. It was a pure, strong episode, different from Bethel, but still completely free from any kind of pains or remembrances, because the indestructible power of humane qualities was made manifest about us by the countless Sudeten and East Germans just beyond being refugees.

I never will forget the church service of the pastor in Siebenbürg in which our whole group participated. The situation was comparable to the American emigration experience. It is, I find, very pronounced in Germany today. One shouldn't talk on and on in Germany in a disparaging vein about Americanization. I see this too; German students of today aren't more brilliant than American students. But emigrants into West Germany have been managed in a way that has my greatest respect; nothing more could be wished for in comparison to the assimilation of emigrants in America. I only fear this success is credited too much to the national sector, as if only Germans had helped Germans. A refugee and emigrant has the right to be accepted whether or not he is welcome. That irrevocable right of the refugee created America and forced the native elements to condescend—yes, the word isn't very pretty—to condescend more and more, to let down the barriers and to stop imagining themselves better than they are.

I find this aspect of the German wonder since 1945 something much greater than the economic wonder. I value the economic wonder only as a means to an end: to accommodate this influx of fourteen million emigrants from the east. I would get along with my German friends and especially with the German public, and Germans would care a little more for Americans, I think, if they didn't brag about their economic capabilities but said instead, "Now we understand Americans. We've carried through a corresponding achievement here. Oh, it was frightful. Many of these people become our competitors in the end; they elbowed for position. But we did our duty. At least we hope we've done our duty." A farmer in Traunreudt said to me, "What a blessing for Bavaria, that these people have come here."

Question: You saw Germany again in 1950. You drew conclusions, then had to go through another separation. Right at the beginning of our conversation you said that you now feel at home in your village. Haven't you ever wished to come back again to Germany?

Answer: You ought not ask. The question ignores the fate of the intellectual strata that emigrated, although they really were completely unable to emigrate, and of the strata that immigrated, although America didn't want any part of its brand of immigration. We are the generation which forces Europe and America together for the first time, which must force them together permanently. What forms will be assumed, only God knows. Only an individual entirely unpretentiously and without anticipating how far along he'll get in his lifetime can propose how the free spaces of America and the thickly clogged canals of Europe may accommodate one another so that the translated life of the mind and spirit of Europe can water and make fruitful these broad expanses of America. I may not give up the captured place in America. I don't know to what extent I can step back and forth over the dividing line. If I were now to simply put behind me these past 25 years, I would not be performing the service to which I know I've been called.

CHAPTER 13

METANOIA: TO THINK ANEW[1]

My dear friend:

You have asked about my "conversion" from a Roman Catholic trend. In these days of Roman "romanticism" you have a right to this question. It is with some reluctance that I set out to describe to you the turning point of my life, after Germany's defeat in 1918. As you will understand at the end, it was precisely that which the Letter to the Hebrews calls "metanoia" from dead works. I cannot well use any English or German term for the event, and I certainly can call it a "conversion" only if you remember the meaning of metanoia.

In order to make the event clear, I must tell you something of the threads of my life which changed their direction by this experience. And I have to apologize if this should prove to you tedious. Although the effort will be to keep the antecedents down to a minimum, a certain confusing pluralism of the facts making up the situation remains a regrettable obstacle for an easy reading. "Metanoia" simplifies life; before, however, lives are the more complex, the richer they are.

The reason why the terms "conversion" and "repentance" do not fit, is a part of the story itself. But it may facilitate your task of understanding what I am driving at, if I say that we all have a double problem on hand, for our faith and for the health of our soul. One is the mental irresolution of deciding whether there is a God, or the Church of Christ, or a living Spirit. The other is the question whether the institutions through which we

[1] A letter to a friend, dated Feb. 18, 1946.

try to express this faith are apt to carry conviction and to absolve us from our duty to witness our faith in new ways.

Most church people consider the first question: does he believe? the paramount question. But my story exclusively centers on the second: are you not cheating yourself when you pretend to believe? For it so happened that I never had any of the apparently general doubts about God, Church, dogma. I cannot remember that I ever could understand why everybody did not believe the Nicean Creed, from about the time I began to think at all. I recall that in my school days I used a German song as an illustration of my faith in the fundamental significance of the incarnation. The song runs: *Es war als haette der Himmel die Erde sanft gekuesst* (It was as though heaven tenderly had kissed the earth). This, I felt, had happened at the beginning of our era. And it seemed very tempting to me even before I joined actively the Church at 18 to think of myself as a future minister of the gospel, and I was startled when my best friend was absolutely incredulous at my telling him so. I thought in my naiveté that this was the normal and natural activity of a man.

But when it comes to the externals of my life before 1918, this, my intellectual attitude, must be implemented by some facts. Externally, ever since I was in school, I had precociously studied history and linguistics, had taken my doctor's degree at the age of 20, was exceedingly proud of the fact that at 23 I had been asked to join the finest law faculty of any university in the world, and had the ambition of being as good a scholar as I could. The idol of scholarship held me firmly in its grip; let us call it charitably the god of the research of truth.

Then there was a second string to my bow. The state in Germany required our service in peace time in its army. Also, I taught its law and constitution and the history of both, since 1912. The government, then the god of law and power, held my allegiance. While I was in the army I discovered a lot about service, comradeship, vice, discipline: that is, good as well as bad things, in myself and others. And in the army the good and the bad is written large so that nobody can overlook either.

The third relation, the relation to the Church, was one of

orthodoxy. Chesterton's "Heretics" and "Orthodoxy" I nearly knew by heart. I took occasion to visit some fine Roman Catholic priests and monks. Cardinal Newman to me was a matter of course. And though I did not yet do much about it, in my thoughts I considered myself on the road to integral "Churchism." My love for the middle ages was an element in this as I began my scientific activity with a study on the medieval liturgy and as I was so much of a historian that the past was romanticized by me too readily. But romanticism was only one and not the most important element in my religious orthodoxy.

For when I had come to the University of Heidelberg at the age of 18, it was the lack of any confessing and living faith there which drove me wild. And the social struggles, especially the unrest in Czarist Russia, and the class warfare in industry, were constantly present to my mind. When some years later a Russian Marxian in Heidelberg announced the coming of the revolution, I advanced a plan of a "moral equivalent for a military army" by starting a work service from all classes of the people. This vision of 1911–12 I developed without any knowledge of William James' ideas. I was surprised to read his paper when I came to this country. The gradual implementation of this plan has taken much of my later life, from my first steps in the army itself to Camp William James in Vermont. But now it is mentioned only to explain that, as an answer to the German defeat in World War I, fortunately the three gods, the god of scholarship, the god of government and law, the god in church, at least had not killed my sensitivity to the real sore spot of our society.

And in 1917 the vision of the revolutions of the Christian world was preying on my mind at the front as I have told in the preface of *Out of Revolution*. In this book the scholar and the historian, the Christian and the man of law and order, all could participate, and the prospect of this book gave me strength, before Germany collapsed. But when this earthquake happened, even the book was engulfed in the vortex. Before I speak of 1918 in detail, I want you to understand that I forbade myself, among other things, to write this very book, although at that time it would have made me famous. It was not before

1931 that the time for a book of scholarship returned for me. In 1918 these glories were renounced.

From 1918 onward I denied myself the satisfaction of following one of the three open trends of the past, in church, science, or state. Why? Well, in 1918 my whole world organized in church, state, universities, the "Western World" that is, collapsed. In the summer of 1918 it dawned on me that the end of German statehood had come. The World War itself (not the so-called World Revolution deliberately staged by the Bolsheviks) was to me the great collapse which Marx and Henry Adams, Nietzsche and Giuseppe Ferrari had foreseen. Germany to me was as amorphous and stateless after 1918 as you must now recognize it to be. Although I prophesied a "pseudo-emperor" for a short later episode, he would not alter the fact that Germany from 1918 on was thrown upon the whole world and could only come to rest as an organized economy within a whole organization of the planet.

Since this was to me self-evident—and I have lived by this self-evidence and never again believed in a sovereign Germany—it was evident that the spiritual powers by which God's Spirit was represented in the German nation as in any other of the West, that is to say the Church, the Government, the institutions of higher learning, all three had piteously failed. They had not been anointed with one drop of the oil of prophecy which God requires from our governors, from our teachers, and from our churches, if they shall act under the grace of God. Not one of them had had any inkling of the doom or any vision for any future beyond mere national sovereignty.

However, God had spoken by events which to be sure went far beyond any one man's arbitrary making, and in these mighty judgements, the three representatives of His Word on earth, the law of nations, the sacramental church, the universities, all three had been obtuse. They had lost their *scent*. And Luke 12:54 ff. was read with pertinent application to our days. *For we do not live by sight but by scent, of which faith is the sublimation.*

To a man of faith in the verdict of God, the three greatest German institutions proved apoplectic. On the surface, they might still function as they did. But to enter the Roman Church now, or to pursue an academic career, or to enter or stay in government service, would have made it impossible to bear witness to God's verdict. Any role in one of these three doomed institutions would have gagged me and therefore at best be meaningless. I would throw my weight behind these institutions simply by going on within them, drawing my salary from them, etc.

And now the strange thing happened which I could not foresee and which makes it seem worthwhile to me that you should receive this letter. These very institutions, all three, in a miraculous rivalry, came to me with tempting offers in the month of November 1918. This dramatized the crisis and made it explicit. The new revolutionary government, the finest flower of the religious press, the university, all three promised me suddenly a meteoric career if I would serve them.

This is what happened. A radical socialist member of the German Reichstag had been placed in my battalion[2] and I had impressed him sufficiently to receive now a wire from him in Berlin, that he would make me undersecretary of the ministry of the Interior to work out the new constitution of the republic. This wire I received at a military hospital, and on November 8th, on the eve of the emperor's abdication on the 9th, I carried this telegram with me on the train to Kassel where I was to take over new orders for joining the front on the 12th. But I carried another offer with me too. In the anguish of my heart, essays had taken shape and had gone to the leading religious magazine of Germany, the "Hochland," which sometimes accepted Protestant contributions. They not only found no lack of orthodoxy in them, but were relieved to publish "Siegfried's Tod", (the death of Siegfried) on November 1, 1918. It was the only timely utterance of some depth, at the downfall of the Reich, and it created a sensation. The editor asked me to hurry to Munich and to help in the sudden catastrophe to fill the magazine with the right kind of nourishment. I had only to hold on to this course and would have

[2] Rudolph Breitscheid. Army Headquarters had devised this scheme so that he be under control.

landed as a well established Roman Catholic religious editor. And then, of course, there was the university with my mighty plan of a history of the Christian revolutions, and with literally thousands of students going to swamp it, to which the faculty expected me to return.

At the railroad junction of Wabern, my wife and I took leave of a minister of the Reformed Church in Barmen who had been at the same hospital. He was a nice man, and I think a Christian, but he had, despite my attempts to tell him, only begun to fathom our crisis. He had enough time before parting to discuss the three opportunities. I first spoke of the chance of writing the new constitution. "Accept," he said. "How useful you can be!" Then I talked glowingly of my prospects in the religious field. Being a minister, he thought that was even better. And then I dangled before his and my eyes all the economic advantages in Leipzig where a university professor in 1914 made about 20,000 dollars (in purchasing power). And the good man again nodded and said that since I was married I should give my academic chances serious consideration.

Then it became clear to me that by accepting any one of these offers I would become a parasite of German defeat. The country was heading towards disrepute, defeat, poverty, and I would get on top of this corpse. I would shine either as undersecretary or a religious editor or as a university teacher. And I would have to wave a flag which had proved to be uninspired, unprophetic, and would make other people believe that I believed in its message when I did not.

I simply went back to the garrison and forgot about my prospects and did my daily chores around the barracks helping to demobilize in great haste the thousands of men. I then went back to my faculty and read an address before the dean and faculty taking by and large Justice Robert Jackson's point of view that a world community could only be constituted by the world's nations taking action against Germany as a state. The paper which was printed then, and today reads as though written for the Nuremberg trials, finished my career in that faculty. Later in 1919 I had occasion to speak before the

Catholic bishop of Wuerzburg and the prevailing Catholic students of that city. I began with St. Paul's word *"scio cui credidi,"* "I know in whom I have believed." It was the Apostle's day in the calendar. But the orthodoxy of my method could not conceal the fact that never would this old priest give me his blessing. And I kept awake all night after that speech, overcome with great pain. And to this day, and I am sure to the end of life, the church to which I hope to belong always will include the Roman, in my heart.

So, instead of church, government, or university, I went into industry. I took a position at the Daimler-Benz automobile factory in Stuttgart. My boss could not make out for a long time what a strange guy he had hired to assist him on labor problems. I parted with my academic library; for worthless paper money, by the way. The buyer sold it to Switzerland for 10,000 gold francs. This then was the turning point of my life. I learned what "Hebrews" meant by metanoia from dead works. If the vehicles of the Spirit are sullied, it's no use disobeying the verdict of history over them. I did probably not advance much in personal virtue by this about face towards the future, away from any visible institution. I did not become a saint. All I received was life. From then on, I had not to say anything which did not originate in my heart. In the process I rediscovered the meaning of original sin. Under original sin the offices which we hold in society force us to think one way and act in another. This chain I had broken. The term "repentance" is absolute nonsense for this decision. The Salvation Army type of repentance confesses one's private and usually perfectly unimportant sins. These private sins occur when we have nothing big to live for.

I emphatically decline to admit that I repented on that November 8, 1918, and in the following period, for my private sins. Perhaps I should, but I did not repent, and I had nothing to repent. I was called into a new, dangerous form of existence *which did not yet exist.* One cannot stress strongly enough the difference between this situation and the sinning against the ten commandments. I was in danger of falling into the sin against the Holy Ghost by doing the dead works of scholarship, state, church. The urgency of the catastrophe challenged me to do repentance not for my sins but for the sin against the Holy Spirit committed and perpetrated by these institutions. The crime or sin against the Holy Spirit always is committed as a social and collective action. And we repent for it by dissociating ourselves from the profession or institution which is God-forsaken.

This dissociation, however, is more easily formulated than achieved. Because no social space or field exists outside the powers that be, and the existing institutions are all there is at the moment of one's metanoia, of one's giving up their dead works. On November 8, 1918, nothing existed except the church, politics, science by which to express one's faith. It takes a lifetime and longer to extricate oneself from the established institutions and to find new ways of establishing some less corrupt forms of expression for the living faith.

Metanoia is not an act of the will. It is the unwillingness to continue. This unwillingness is not an act but an experience. The words make no sense, the atmosphere is stifled. One chokes. One has no choice but to leave. But one does not know what is going to happen, one has no blue-print for action. The "decision" literally means what it means in Latin, the being-cut-off from one's own routines in a paid and honored position. And the trust that this subzero situation is bound to create new ways of life is our faith.

It seems necessary to remind people that this is the way of salvation experienced by any new-born souls and that God seems to care little for the problem of smoking or drinking or similar secondary matters. Because the sins against the Holy Ghost are the only ones which cannot be forgiven. The others are important for the immature. This one alone counts in the course of God's history of salvation for grown up people.

I have never written down the story of my "metanoia" before as all my later life grew out of this and has kept me pretty busy. But since you have asked me point blank, I seemed to owe you an answer. And now I have looked back upon that moment at the railroad junction of Wabern and reflected that it draws attention to the original sense of the decision a

Christian was asked to make in the old days: to distinguish the spirits of death and life, and to turn away from dead works although they might be sanctified by the highest authority. Because God is a God of the living and His judgements may be expected any day.

Very sincerely your friend,

Eugen Rosenstock-Huessy

APPENDIX

Diagrams of The Ka

(see Chapter 3)

1.

2.

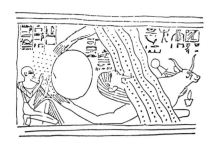

3.

4.

Biography of Eugen Rosenstock-Huessy

Eugen Rosenstock-Huessy was born in Berlin, Germany in 1888, the son of a Jewish banker. After receiving his doctorate in law from Berlin University, he taught law at Leipzig University from 1912 to 1914. In the First World War he was an officer at the front near Verdun.

During the war he and his friend Franz Rosenzweig conducted an extended correspondence on Judaism and Christianity. Rosenstock-Huessy, who had embraced Christianity as a young man, had almost convinced his friend Rosenzweig to do the same. Their letters, first published in the 1920's, have been widely commented on as a classic contemporary confrontation between Christian and Jew.

In 1914 he married Margrit Huessy and added his wife's surname to his own in the Swiss custom. After the war he did not return to the university but instead went to work for Daimler-Benz at their Stuttgart automobile manufacturing plant. There, in 1919–21, he founded and edited the first factory magazine in Germany. In 1921–22 he founded and headed The Academy of Labor at Frankfurt, a pioneering effort in adult education. Later, in 1929, he was elected chairman of the World Association for Adult Education.

He returned to university life in 1923, as professor of law at the University of Breslau. In 1924 he published *Angewandte Seelenkunde* (*An Applied Science of the Soul*), his first formulation of a proposed method for the social sciences, a method based on speech. This was followed in 1925 by an elaborated formulation of the method in a book entitled *Soziologie*. When his Roman Catholic friend, Joseph Wittig, was excommunicated, he wrote with him a book on church history, *Das Alter der Kirche* (*The Age of the Church*), and published it in 1928.

While at Breslau, in 1928–30, he organized voluntary work

service camps which brought together workers, farmers and students in work together on the land. This and his subsequent similar activities in the United States have been described as forerunners of the Peace Corps.

In 1931 he published a major historical work, *Die Europäischen Revolutionen* (*The European Revolutions*), a book which established his reputation in Europe. A completely rewritten version of this book was published in the United States in 1938 as *Out of Revolution*.

Immediately after Hitler came to power in 1933, he voluntarily left Germany and went to the United States. After teaching two years at Harvard, he joined the faculty at Dartmouth College where he taught as professor of social philosophy until his retirement in 1957.

With the backing of President Franklin Roosevelt, in 1940 he organized an experimental camp within the Civilian Conservation Corps. Camp William James in Tunbridge, Vermont was experimental in that it was to train leaders for a possible development of the CCC into a service that would accept volunteers from all walks of life, not simply young men in need of work.

He continued to write throughout the period 1940 to 1960, publishing *The Christian Future* in 1945 and a much expanded *Soziologie* in two volumes in 1956–8. The second volume is a universal history of man interpreted in the spirit of the new method which is the subject of volume one. In 1963 he published a major work on speech and the relation of speech to his method, *Die Sprache des Menschengeschlechts* (*The Speech of Mankind*).

During the 1950's he lectured at the German universities of Göttingen, Berlin and Münster. In the 1960's he lectured in the United States at Columbia and California. He lives in the Norwich, Vermont home to which he came in 1937.

Bibliography

I. Books Currently in Print by Eugen Rosenstock-Huessy

(The following are all available from Argo Books, Inc., Norwich, Vt. 05055.)

In English:

Bibliography-Biography. Four Wells, 1959, 38 pp., Hardbound.
The Christian Future. Harper, 1966, 248 pp., Paperback.
I Am an Impure Thinker. Argo, 1969, 200 pp., Paperback and Hardbound.
Judaism Despite Christianity (Exchange of letters with Franz Rosenzweig). University of Alabama Press, 1969, 198 pp., Hardbound.
The Multiformity of Man. Beachhead, 1948, 70 pp., Paperback.
Out of Revolution. Argo, 1969, 795 pp., Paperback.
Speech and Reality. Argo, 1969, 200 pp., Paperback and Hardbound.

In German:

Des Christen Zukunft. Siebenstern, 1965, 350 pp., Paperback.
Dienst auf dem Planeten. Kohlhammer, 1965, 176 pp., Paperback.
Die Europäischen Revolutionen und der Charakter der Nationen. Kohlhammer, 1961, 584 pp., Hardbound.
Frankreich-Deutschland. Vogt, 1957, 108 pp., Hardbound.
Das Geheimnis der Universität. Kohlhammer, 1958, 320 pp., Paperback.
Ja und Nein. Lambert Schneider, 1968, 180 pp., Paperback.
Königshaus und Stämme. Scientia, 1965, 418 pp., Hardbound.
Die Sprache des Menschengeschlechts, Bd. I. Lambert Schneider, 1963, 810 pp., Hardbound.

Die Sprache des Menschengeschlechts, Bd. II. Lambert Schneider, 1964, 903 pp., Hardbound.

Soziologie—Bd. I. Die Übermacht der Räume. Kohlhammer, 1956, 336 pp., Hardbound.

Soziologie—Bd. II. Die Vollzahl der Zeiten. Kohlhammer, 1958, 774 pp., Hardbound.

Die Umwandlung. Lambert Schneider, 1968, 140 pp., Paperback.

Der Unbezahlbare Mensch. Herder, 1964, 173 pp., Paperback.

Zurück in das Wagnis der Sprache. Vogt, 1957, 82 pp., Hardbound.

NOTE: In addition to the above, there are currently available a number of booklets and tape recordings by Eugen Rosenstock-Huessy. A supplementary listing of these works may be obtained from Argo Books.

II. Books by Rosenstock-Huessy Not Currently in Print

(The following is a selective bibliography. A complete bibliography as of 1958 is available in the books *Bibliography-Biography* and *Das Geheimnis der Universität* listed above.)

Das Alter der Kirche. (Mit Joseph Wittig.) Berlin: Lambert Schneider, 1927–28, 3 Vols., 1,250 pp.

Das Arbeitslager. Jena: E. Diedrichs, 1931, 159 pp.

Der Atem des Geistes. Frankfurt: Verlag der Frankfurter Hefte, 1951, 294 pp.

Heilkraft und Wahrheit. Stuttgart: Evangelisches Verlagswerk, 1952, 215 pp.

Die Hochzeit des Krieges und der Revolution. Würzburg: Patmos, 1920, 306 pp.

Im Kampf um die Erwachsenbildung. Leipzig: Quelle & Meyer, 1926, 240 pp.

Industrierecht. Berlin: H. Sack, 1926, 183 pp.

Werkstattaussiedlung. Berlin: J. Springer, 1922, 286 pp.

INDEX

Abraham, 169
abstraction, 78; *abstractum*, 55, 58, 59
acquired faculties, 69, 70
acts, 85–90, 97; action, 80, 112
Adam, 61, 95, 117
Adams, John Quincy, 75
Adams, Henry, 22, 185
adulthood, 74
Ammon, Jakob, 105; Amish Men, 105, 106
analysis, 49, 56
analytics, 58
anarchy, 17, 18
ancestor, 123, 127, 132, 135; ancestor worship, 122; ancestry, 126
Anselm of Canterbury, 1, 14
anticipation, 98, 109
Antioch College, 98
antiquity, 115, 116, 135, 138, 139
Ares, 85
aristocrat, 144, 145, 158; aristocracy, 137, 139, 146, 147, 151, 164
Aristotle (384–322 B.C.), 119, 137, 138
army, 183, 184
art, 167
artist(s), 118, 178
Artemis, 84, 85
atheism, 103; atheist(s), 19, 173

articulation, 55, 58, 63
astrologer, 115, 118
Atum (god), 38
Augustine, St., bishop of Hippo, 133, 134
authority(ies), 27, 121, 123, 124, 125, 128

Bach, Johann Sebastian (1685–1750), 150, 167
Bastille, 154
Beethoven, Ludwig von, 118, 167
Bergson, Henri, 26, 93
"being", 3, 78, 80–87, 90, 151
Bethel, 179, 180
Bible, 29, 70, 159; Lutheran —, 169
biology, 3, 4, 106; biologist, 16
bionomics, 4, 5, 164
birth, 94, 123, 126, 132; virgin —, 158
Bodelschwingh, Friedrich von, 179
body(ies), 3, 5–7, 15, 23, 77, 99, 108, 112, 116; — of space, 116, 123, 130; — of time, 119, 127, 128, 153, 156
Bohr, Niels (1885–1969), 157
Boleyn, Anne, 163
Bolsheviks, 140, 144, 147, 157, 160, 185
Bonaventura (1221–1274), 67, 68
bourgeois, 142, 144, 145, 148